Privileged
To Live

A Mother's Story of Survival

Verna   Griffin

MILLIGAN BOOKS   BOOKS   CALIFORNIA

Printed and Bound in the United States of America
Published and Distributed by:
Milligan Books, Inc.

Cover Layout by Mario M. Rodriguez
Interior Design by Caldonia Joyce
First Printing, May 2005
10987654321

ISBN: 0-9767678-6-4

Milligan Books
1425 W. Manchester Blvd., Suite C
Los Angeles, CA 90047

www.milliganbooks.com
drrosie@aol.com
(323) 750-3592

Dedication

I dedicate this book to my family. **Family is Gold** is our motto.

To all who have had shattered dreams, dashed hopes, and thwarted plans and have given up somewhere down the line, I dedicate this book with hopes that it will encourage you not to give up and to firmly believe that there is still hope.

To parents: Don't ever forsake your children. Those same children may have to take care of *you* someday.

Table of Contents

Acknowledgments

Special thanks to:

My parents, Matthew and Roberta Silverson, for their spiritual guidance and support in every way.

My grandparents who gave me the opportunity to know them and enjoy them. Without them, there would not have been future generations.

My son Andre Young for never giving up on his mom through all the hard times and for sharing, caring, giving support, and giving me the opportunity to write this story.

My daughter Shameka Crayon for staying close to me and offering her support whenever I needed a hand in every way possible.

My son Tyree Crayon who is deceased, but his spirit seems to continue to carry me through hard times.

My sisters-in-law, Johnnie Young and Elaine Goodman, who remain a part of my family and are always there for me, as well as for their nieces and nephews.

My grandchildren, La Tonya, La Toya, Tyra, Ashley, Cedric, Curtis, Marcel, Tyler, Kion, Summer, Truice, Truly, Andre Jr., King and Kaylon for making my life something so grand.

My great-grandchildren, Kani'ya, Amir, and Tatiyana, who made my life even more meaningful to be able to live to see great-grands.

All of my uncles, aunts, and cousins who have offered their encouraging words.

All of my friends whom I grew up with and still remain close in my life.

Mrs. Bobbie Hogue for recognizing the possibility of my life story becoming a book and encouraging me to write.

I would also like to thank Ms. Elizabeth Morgan, Mr. Wright, and all the wonderful people who had input in the completion of this book.

Gracie and Silas Green (my mom's parents) and Hattie Silverson (my dad's mom).

CHAPTER 1

My Family History

It has been said that "Talent isn't born; it's created." But, I believe that there are those rare occasions where talent *is* born. As I look back over my life, my children's lives, and the lives of the generations before us, it seems to me that the foundation of our successes is rooted in a number of inborn qualities: the determination to do what we set out to do, despite obstacles; a caring and sharing attitude that shows a willingness to do for others; and the courage to make sacrifices and know the importance of a strong family bond. These traits have been passed down in our family for many generations. What other explanation could there be for four generations of gifted individuals in my family?

These traits were first evident in my grandparents, Silas and Gracie Green, seemingly plain and simple Black folk who lived in Waskom, Texas. Gracie was born in Greenwood, Louisiana, and Silas was born in Waskom. Both of my grandparents came from large families. Silas was one of nine children; Gracie, one of ten. As small towns go, they probably knew each other growing up and were likely childhood sweethearts. After marrying in 1909, Silas and Gracie moved to Waskom, where all of their eleven children were born. My grandfather was a striking, strong-willed young man of medium height and dark skin, with a heart of gold. My grandmother was a very fair-skinned lady, who proudly strutted when she walked.

Like many Black families of their day, my grandparents worked on white people's land in exchange for a place to stay. They were required to give the landowners a portion of the crops that they grew. This was known as *sharecropping*.

Silas and Gracie were not like most sharecroppers, who typically were poor and barely made a living. They were blessed with a kind and generous landlord who only required that they hand over to him three bales of cotton a year. Beyond that, they were allowed to keep everything that they grew.

Silas and Gracie were hardworking people. They produced far more than the three bales per year required by the landlord and were, therefore, able to reap tremendous profits. Aside from growing cotton, they also owned a syrup-producing sugar mill, raised their own farm animals, and grew other crops.

Realizing that everyone was not as fortunate as they were, Silas and Gracie were very generous people, who gladly shared their abundant crops and goods with other sharecroppers. My grandparents were extraordinary people. Only after seeing to it that the family's needs were met did my grandparents sell their excess products.

My grandmother was a talented dressmaker. This proved to be especially beneficial to the family because nine of the eleven children were girls. Gracie would spot a dress at a store in town, buy the fabric, go home, and duplicate the dress exactly. She also made shirts for her husband and the two boys.

My grandfather was what many would call a *jack-of-all-trades*. He was highly skilled and respected throughout the community. He was a butcher. The meat that he didn't give his family and others, he sold in town. He also helped lay the crossties for railroad tracks and was skilled at making wagon wheels. He even assisted in preparing bodies for burial. I remember as a little girl, hearing my mom and my aunt telling stories about how coins were placed on the deceased's eyes to keep them closed and how the body had to be strapped down in order to lay straight.

My grandfather was also a respected member of the church and assisted the preacher with baptisms.

The landlord's generosity, coupled with a strong work ethic, allowed my grandparents to maintain a better lifestyle than most of the other Black families in the small Texas town of Waskom. The Greens lived in a wood-framed, unpainted house, which was quite typical of the family dwellings in the early 1900s. The house had three large bedrooms, a large living room that doubled as a bedroom, a dining room, and a kitchen. A double fireplace heated two of the bedrooms; a wood-burning heater warmed the living room. The family owned a car, a Victrola record player, and a very large collection of 78 records.

The Greens began teaching their children the value of hard work at an early age. All the children had chores. The girls shared the housework, which included washing the dishes, washing and ironing clothes, and milking the cows. The two boys performed outdoor duties, such as chopping wood and feeding livestock.

The children stuck close together. They went to and from school together, played together, and prayed together as faithful members of Union Chapel Baptist Church.

At one point in their life, my grandparents' faith was clearly tested. Their connection to God and the church was their saving grace. Prior to that time, two of the Greens' children had become sick and died.

After that, they were prepared to lose their youngest daughter when she came down with a mysterious illness that baffled the doctors, who told them to prepare for Roberta's death. The thought of losing Roberta was devastating to Silas and Gracie.

Bedridden, Roberta couldn't eat or drink and was completely nonresponsive. Then one miraculous day, things began to change. Roberta's oldest brother Bob went into her room, knelt down by her side, pried her parched lips apart, and forced a teaspoon of water into her slightly opened mouth. The water trickled past her lips and slowly went down her throat. Moments later, Roberta began to show signs of life. From that moment, she slowly recovered.

To this day, no one really knows what made Roberta sick. But her survival ensured a future generation of offspring and kept alive the legacy of successful people originating from her parents. In fact, like her mother, Roberta had the gift of sewing and would later become a hardworking seamstress.

Years later, all of Silas and Gracie's children married and moved away with the exception of Roberta and an older sister, Essie. The four of them stayed in their Texas home until a 1945 chimney fire caused the house to burn to the ground. After salvaging what little was left, they moved to a new house up the road. Soon thereafter, Essie got married, leaving Roberta as the only remaining sibling in the household.

In 1949, my grandparents' oldest daughter, Nellie, who was married and living in Los Angeles, California, sent for them to come live with her and her husband, Julian. After moving to California, Lola, one of Roberta's sisters, suggested that Roberta come live with her and her husband and two children in San Pedro, California. Lola, a free spirit, worked in the garment industry; her husband, Jesse, worked at Ford Motors.

This Picture is taken of my Mom, three of her Sisters, her Nieces and Nephew. This was taken on the side of the wood framed house they grew up in. Top from left to right: Essie, Lola Roberta. Roberta's nieces and nephew at bottom, and oldest sister, Hettie sits in the window.

CHAPTER 2

My Parents

During her stay at Lola's house, Roberta met Mr. Leslie Spratt, a friend of Lola's husband. A romance blossomed between the two. From this union, I was born Verna Jean Spratt, on February 4, 1949, in the Seaside Memorial Hospital, at Long Beach, California. My father abandoned my mother when he learned that she was pregnant. He insisted that the child wasn't his. He was never involved in my life. He completely missed out on the opportunity to raise his beautiful daughter. My mother attempted, on several occasions, to get him to live up to his responsibilities, but to no avail. He agreed to pay her hospital bill, but he never did.

My mother soon realized that she had no choice but to raise me as a single parent. After leaving the hospital, she took me to Lola's house to live. With a screaming, six pound five ounce newborn who needed food and many other things, my mother quickly realized that she needed to contribute financially to her sister's household. So, she set out to find a job.

Finding work was not an easy task. But finally, after many rejections, Roberta found a job at A-1 Kotzin Manufacturing Company, a producer of men's trousers. My mother worked as a piece worker there for 33 years, making very little money. But, like her parents, she was a living testimony. She worked hard, seldom missing a day's work. In fact, she would sometimes go to work sick, just so she could earn enough to make ends meet.

As fate would have it, Roberta met a man at work. This man would be the only father I would ever know.

Early one evening after a long, hard day at work, the attendant, Matthew Silverson, approached Roberta as she walked through the parking lot at Twelfth and Maple. My mother was a beautiful woman with a caramel complexion, a slender frame, and a jaunty strut. Her natural pride was evident in the way she walked. Roberta stopped to hear what Mr. Silverson had to say. He later stated, "I knew I had her when she stopped." And he did. On June 10, 1950, Roberta

Green and Matthew Silverson were united in holy matrimony.

Shortly after the wedding, Matthew Silverson adopted me, and I became Verna Jean Silverson. We moved into a little place on Newton Street, close to downtown Los Angeles, near the Newton Street Police Station. Our new home was a boarding house where many visitors came and went.

Several things about this home and its surrounding neighborhood left an impression on me. For instance, I always looked forward to seeing Mr. Lloyd, the iceman, who delivered ice twice a week for our icebox, which was the forerunner to the more modern refrigerator. I still remember the monumental entrances he made. When he appeared in the doorway, he would block the light behind him until he stepped into the house. Mr. Lloyd was a robust man who wore an old, worn, heavy cloth jacket, very high wet boots, and a big, black, rubber apron around his neck, which also appeared to be quite heavy. After he grasped the ice with a pair of giant steel tongs, he would flip it with ease in one smooth motion over his shoulder onto his back. Like a giant, uncut diamond glistening in the light, he carried the ice up our stairs into our one-room flat and laid it to rest at the bottom of the icebox.

I was amazed that that one block of ice would keep the food in the large, metal box cold for three to four days until the iceman came again. My dad had the thankless job of emptying the metal pan under the icebox after it had filled with water that dripped from the melting ice. When Mr. Lloyd would leave, my mom always said, "Thank you so much; see you next time." As soon as he got outside, I would hear him yell, "Iceman!" as he continued his rounds.

Just as intriguing to me as the iceman, was seeing the interesting people who frequented the boarding house, some of whom were rather friendly. We lived in one room, which served as our bedroom, kitchen, and social place. I could hear just about every noise in the hallway. I had to walk down the hall on the creaky, wooden floor to get to the common bathroom shared by all the tenants. I recall seeing the dingy fixtures and smelling old urine seeping into the hallway from the bathroom. The smell may also have come from the floorboards (when tenants didn't make it to the bathroom).

When I got the opportunity to get out of the house, I would go through the back gate of the boarding house and cross the alley to my Aunt Nellie's back gate. I went there often to visit my cousin, Lawrence, their younger child. I thought it was great to be able to get to Aunt Nellie's house so easily. Unlike us, Aunt Nellie and Uncle Julian owned their house.

Lawrence had an older sister named Annie who did not live at the house for very long after we moved to California. From what I recall, Annie was busty and hippy. I was a frail child in comparison and often wished I had a figure like hers.

At times, I would stand on the side of Uncle Julian's old car and watch my reflection in the car grow short and wide as I moved back and forth. When I did this, I would imagine myself looking like Annie someday.

Aunt Nellie was a great cook. She could bake a *mean* pineapple-coconut layer cake. Every time she would bake one, I would eat it until I was full. Uncle Julian was known for drinking lots of Pepsi-Colas, so much so that people called him a *Pepsi-holic*. I could always count on being offered a Pepsi during my visits.

I loved visiting Lawrence because he told fabulous stories about his experiences in a gang called *The Businessmen*. They were one of the most notorious gangs in the L.A. area at that time. His gang activity landed him in and out of jail. In fact, he spent much of his life in California's correctional facilities. Nevertheless, he was still one of my favorite childhood cousins. I loved visiting him and hearing about his wild and illicit adventures.

Lawrence had a very large collection of 45 records, which very few people other than me knew about. He was extremely proud and protective of his collection. Not even I could touch any of the 45s without his permission. I am not sure what the consequences would have been had I touched them, but I never wanted to find out, either. If I wanted to hear a record, he would say, "Don't touch it! I will play it for you."

Lawrence was as protective of me as he was of his records. That's why I loved him so much. He made me feel special. At the same time, he was pretty rough to play with occasionally. He liked to use me as a punching bag. At first, it seemed harmless, but one summer day, that rough treatment became serious. During a discussion, I disagreed with something he had said, and then all hell broke loose. He snapped and started hitting me so hard that I wound up on the floor beside the bed in Aunt Nellie's bedroom. Then Lawrence jumped on top of me, put his hands around my throat, and began choking me. I felt like I was going to pass out.

At that point, I reached under the bed and grabbed one of my Uncle Julian's steel-toed boots and began swinging it. I managed to clobber him in the forehead. It must have hurt him pretty badly because from that day forward, he never even raised his hand to hit me, although he continued to threaten to hurt anyone who wanted to harm me. Despite that incident, I continued to adore him through the good and the bad.

At one point, my mom hired a baby-sitter for me. Her name was Mrs. Farley; she lived around the corner from Lawrence, near 14th and Hooper streets. Mrs. Farley was straight from the "old school." She was very old fashioned and rigid. A dark-skinned lady of medium height and build, Mrs. Farley was about fifty years of age. She wore a short black wig over her natural hair, which was gray and very nappy.

What I remember most clearly about her was her very ugly habit of dipping snuff. This habit seemed quite out of character for Mrs. Farley, who was otherwise quite a neat person, and who always wore a freshly pressed apron. Mrs. Farley's house was immaculate; her insistence on neatness was as rigid as her personality.

On the other hand, Mrs. Farley's husband, who was a slightly overweight, brown-skinned man, was extremely mild-mannered. The Farleys appeared to have very little in common. I didn't see them talking to each other very much. They slept in different rooms: hers was in the front part of the house; his was in the back of the house. They had no children.

In the evenings, Mr. Farley would emerge from his bedroom to eat and watch late-night television. He would often sit on the front porch to water his seemingly perfectly green grass. Mr. Farley spent most of his days at the pool hall at 12th and Central. I would often accompany Mrs. Farley downtown to the Grand Central Market to buy groceries and other goodies. On our way, we would sometimes stop by the pool hall. Because it was a warm, friendly place, I could understand why Mr. Farley preferred it to his home.

Although I was not the only child the Farleys kept on a daily basis, I was the only one who stayed there overnight during the week. My dad decided that it was easier to leave me there all week rather than pick me up nightly. I was just two years old when I began staying at the Farleys' house. Everything had been pretty good in my life *until then*.

Matthew Silverson, my adopted father, played a significant role in my life. Every female child needs a father figure in her life. My adopted father was a tall, slender, dark-skinned man, who enjoyed making people laugh. Growing up in Little Rock, Arkansas, he was one of seven children—five boys and two girls—born to Thomas and Hattie Silverson. Because he felt the need to work to help support his family, his education ended at sixth grade. He lacked the ability to read, but could map out directions to get anywhere he wanted to go. He was also excellent at figuring numbers. He would add bills and other necessities on Friday mornings; cash his check Friday evenings; shop for groceries; come home and count out the money for bills and for our savings; get dressed to meet his brothers—and we would not see him again until early Sunday morning. My father believed that credit was a black man's survival kit; therefore, he paid his bills on time. I don't think my parents were ever late making payments on any of their bills.

Aside from my father's regular weekend habits, he often took his family on outings. Church was our #1 outing, and after church, Dad would treat us to some simple forms of enjoyment. This included visiting family, going to a carnival located on Firestone Street, taking a ride to the city of Wilmington, where we frequented our favorite hamburger stand called Pop's, located on D Street, or getting an ice cream at 76th and San Pedro Street. Occasionally we would pack a lunch for an all-day fishing trip down at Cabrillo Beach.

As I look back, I realize that my mother was a very strong, understanding, and tolerant woman. How she could kiss my father good-bye on Friday night and not see him again until early Sunday morning for years was a mystery to me. When asked where Matthew was, she would simply say, "He's on his mission." I never heard or saw my parents argue or fight, although I would sometimes see my mother saddened by my father's constant weekend excursions. I think she felt that she owed my father a great deal of gratitude. After all, he adopted her only child and treated me as if I was his own. She and I are very thankful for that. Through it all, I can truly say my father was a hardworking man. He not only worked on a regular daytime job, but he also worked various evening jobs. He was an excellent provider for his family.

Matthew and Roberta Silverson (1972).

CHAPTER 3

Life with Mrs. Farley

For some reason, Mrs. Farley treated me differently than the other children. I was the scapegoat for everything that went wrong in the Farley household. I was often blamed and harshly punished for things that I did not do. Many times, I was subjected to Mrs. Farley calling me names such as "little frail pigeon-toed girl." She often told me that I was good-for-nothing and would swat me with a switch from her peach tree.

Most times when Mrs. Farley whipped me, she would grab my dress from the bottom and pull it over my head. Then she whipped me with one hand, while holding the dress together with the other. My arms and hands, as well as my head, were totally enclosed in my dress. I couldn't even attempt to block any of the blows or, for that matter, even see them coming. It was a horrible way to spank a child. I could only cry and scream inside the enclosed chamber of fabric for what seemed to be a lifetime before Mrs. Farley decided my punishment was over.

The only escape I had from this harsh treatment was in the Farleys' backyard. It was a very small yard with a well-manicured flower garden, a large peach tree, and an old shed. The backyard stopped where a huge brick wall of a local factory began. The house had a high, wooden back porch. It was so high that I could actually stand under it as a small child. In that back-yard, I would dream of being a dancer, an actress, or someone famous. I dreamed that my mom and dad were so proud of me because of what I had become. Most of all, I dreamed of getting away from Mrs. Farley forever.

When I was about four years old, we moved to a house on 85th Street, near McKinley Street. We lived in the back house while a family that had three boys lived in the front house. When I would come home from the Farleys' on weekends, my parents would sometimes allow me to play with the boys. Those boys really liked to fight. One of them had a bad habit of spitting on me. When he did that, I would usually wind up running into my house, crying, which brought an end to our playing, at least for the day.

On one occasion, my cousin, Lawrence, who was visiting, was standing on the stairs of the apartment building next door. My mom had obviously told him about the trouble I was having with the boys. While I was playing with the three boys, Lawrence decided to issue a warning to prevent any further spitting. He threatened to throw a big stick down on them if they hit me or spit on me again. They took one look at his hefty size and ran into their house. They would stick their heads out the door from time to time to ask if my cousin was gone yet. After that, they treated me differently, although they still sometimes got the urge to hit me. Mom told me that the next time I was hit, I had better hit back. She had grown tired of me coming home crying and vowed to spank me if it ever happened again. From that day forward, whenever I was hit, I fought back.

At some point, my grandparents moved nearby on 87th Place, near Central Avenue. Mom and I often walked to their house. My grandmother would fix something special for us to eat. My favorite was hot, homemade biscuits with lots of butter and jelly. My grandfather would sometimes take me to the grocery store to buy my favorite foods, such as grapes or raisins.

We spent a lot of time together as a family. My mom and four of her siblings would often get together at my grandparents' house. They would sit around, talking and laughing about the old times. The radio was always set to stations that played New Orleans-style or country music. I remember hearing songs such as "Sixteen Tons" and "Jambalaya."

The family's songs of joy and laughter turned to tears as we were confronted with losing one of our strongest members. I had grown very fond of my grandparents. I was devastated when my grandfather became terminally ill and had to be hospitalized. I can remember how spooky my cousins and I felt on the night we went to visit him. Because he was dying, the hospital allowed us children to visit. As we entered his room, Grandpa was lying in bed with many tubes attached to his body. His breathing was deep with heavy jolts. The machines that were keeping him alive made rhythmical noises. I don't think Grandpa was even aware that we were even in the room. It was very hard to see him, a man whom I had always known as a strong and hardworking person, lying there in that condition, helpless and oblivious to his surroundings. I don't recall anyone saying a word on the way home from the hospital. Everyone's face seemed to say the same thing: We were sad because we knew Grandpa was going to die soon.

The following morning, on April 5, 1954, at 8:45, we got the call that Grandpa had died. As a five-year-old, I had many questions because death was still a mystery to me. After all, I had only felt love from my relatives, my grandparents, my mom, and others. I just could not understand why God would take any of them away from me. My mom, with all her compassion, tried her best to explain it to me, but I still was confused and saddened by my grandpa's death. The thought of never being able to see Grandpa again was just so hard for me to accept and understand.

I remember the funeral as if it were yesterday. Before the service began, most of the people who were dressed in black milled around in front of the church. A long, black limousine was parked in front. Inside the church front and center was a long, decorated box, which contained my grandpa's body. When the service first began, it seemed like any other Sunday church service—until the part when we all walked toward the open box. As everyone walked around, they seemed to be looking as if they were watching him sleep. When it came my time to look at him, an eerie feeling came over me. To me, the man in the box looked nothing like my grandpa. His face was swollen, his lips wrinkled, and he looked very ashy. I started crying when I realized that my mom was crying. I could not bear to see her cry.

After the service, we all got in the long, black cars and rode for what seemed like forever until we finally came to a big, gated yard that people referred to as the cemetery. It was a place I had never seen before with lots of statues and monuments. I soon learned that this was the place where my grandpa would be lowered into a deep hole in the ground forever. Losing Grandpa made me so sad, I could barely face the thought of it. But, I wanted to be strong for my mom and my grandma. It was really hard to leave my grandpa there in a hole in the ground. At that point in my young life, death did not make any sense to me.

Later that night, my cousin Annie and I slept in the living room on a rollaway bed because our grown relatives took all the other beds. Even with all those people around me, I still had very bad dreams that caused me to sometimes wake up, screaming. I realized that I was disturbing everybody in the house, but I couldn't help it. I couldn't get my grandpa's face in that box out of my mind. It was just so frightening.

Days, even weeks, later, I continued to have problems sleeping at night, especially at Mrs. Farley's house, because the room where I slept was always so dark. I would sleep with my head under the cover because I didn't want to see my grandpa's face, which by then, in my mind, had turned into *the monster in a box.*

Not too long after my grandfather's death, my parents were blessed to be able to buy their first house, located on 130th Street. I was excited about having a house with a yard that we didn't have to share with anyone else. Friday was my favorite day of the week because that was when my parents would pick me up from the Farleys'. I'd spend Friday evenings sitting on the Farleys' front porch, anxiously awaiting my parents to pull into the driveway. While I waited, I would count the other cars, wishfully claiming the ones that I hoped to own someday. Just as soon as I spotted my parents' car, I would spring to my feet, run into the house shouting, "My mom is here! My mom is here!" Then I would rush to grab my bag and say good-bye to Mrs. Farley. I moved so fast that I would be ready to jump into the backseat just as soon as the car stopped. Not only did I enjoy being away from Mrs. Farley, but I also liked being with my family on weekends.

We would make many stops on Friday evening. First, we would go to the grocery store. All of us took part in choosing items we liked and needed for the upcoming week, including weekend goodies. When we got home, I would run into my bedroom, put my things away, and rejoin my parents in the kitchen to help put away the groceries. In those days, people took their groceries home in boxes, not the bags we use nowadays. After we did that, I enjoyed playing in the boxes. I converted them into many things: cars, skates, and houses. In the end, I would fall into them, tearing them up. My family would end the evening by watching television together.

I felt like I had the most special family, a family who lived in the most special house in the world. Most of the day on Saturday, I spent time enjoying the serenity of my backyard. It was large and filled with peach trees and flowers of all kinds. It was truly a haven for butterflies. I would get up early on Saturdays, eat breakfast, and then go straight to the backyard with my butterfly jar in tow. This jar was nothing special. It was any ol' jar I could find. I'd punch holes in the top of it so that the butterflies would have air. In a day, I could practically fill my jar with butterflies. They remain one of my favorite creatures on earth. To me, they are the most unique things God ever created. The idea of something as horrendous as a furry worm going into a cocoon and coming out as a beautiful butterfly fascinated me then and still does today. I typically spent the rest of the day playing with the neighborhood kids, something I didn't get to do at Mrs. Farley's house.

Uncle Julian, Lawrence, and Aunt Nellie.

This is a picture taken on my fifth birthday. I'm the little girl in the white long dress with the bow in my hair. Lawrence is in the background in the white shirt. The others are neighborhood children.

CHAPTER 4

School Days

But all too soon it would be Sunday—the D-Day of my life—the day of the week I dreaded the most. Although it was not the worst day, I knew Sunday meant another week would begin at Mrs. Farley's, and I didn't look forward to it.

The morning would start off fine. We attended Sunday school, where we were taught good lessons. Then we participated in a glorious morning worship at the Providence Baptist Church. Because I was a child, I didn't understand and probably didn't listen to what was being said in the sermon. I did, however, enjoy the choir. While the choir didn't sing in perfect harmony, they were good enough to get a few hands clapping and feet patting. Every now and then, they would even inspire a few happy souls to jump up and shout. All the excitement that the singing generated kept me awake. It was another story when the preaching started, however. As soon as the sermon began, I'd find myself dazing, dozing, squirming, and checking my little Mickey Mouse wristwatch.

Some of the traditions of the church were confusing to me, as they probably were to most children my age. I had more questions than I got answers. For instance, I really didn't understand the offering thing or *tithes*, as they were frequently referred to in church. In my young mind, I thought, *If we are giving to God by putting our money in the plate, how does the money get to God?* And if people were blessed for giving a small percentage of their income to the church, I wondered if doctors and lawyers, who made lots of money, received more blessings than poor people on welfare. I worried about whether I would receive any blessings. After all, like most children my age, I had nothing to tithe. Most of the time when I asked such questions, the answers I received left me even more confused. Understand that I was a very curious child who had lots of questions about lots of things. I anxiously waited for the day I would go to school so that I would find some answers to the many questions that plagued me.

I also wondered why pictures of Jesus in the Bible looked different from the Bible's description of the way Jesus was supposed to have looked. I wondered what the Easter bunny had to do with the Resurrection of Christ on Easter Sunday. Did rabbits only lay eggs once a year? Most of all, I wondered what the fat man in the red suit had to do with the birth of Christ. How were the mountains created? How were the stars placed so perfectly in the sky? The universe seemed so amazing and so perfect. Even at that age, I came to the conclusion that a Supreme Being must have created the universe. This early belief has remained with me all my life. It has helped me overcome some of the most difficult obstacles and helped me to remain focused on my life's dreams.

In September 1955, the day had finally arrived when I was old enough to attend school. My parents enrolled me in the 20th Street School in Los Angeles. I had looked forward to going to school for so long because it would be the beginning of getting answers to all of my questions. To my surprise and disappointment, my first day of kindergarten was terrible. . . .

I was nervous and scared. I cried because I didn't want to stay with all those strangers. The teacher either didn't understand my situation, or she was just impatient, because she scorned me for my behavior. To make matters worse, the other children in my classroom made fun of me.

They teased me because of the way I looked. I was very pigeon-toed and had to wear corrective shoes. And, Mrs. Farley always braided my hair in five little braids because she claimed that would make my hair grow. All the other girls wore cute hairstyles, pretty dresses, and fashionable shoes. I never liked the way Mrs. Farley dressed me. I thought she went out of her way to make me look as unattractive as possible. After complaining to my mom, I finally got a pair of black and white saddle oxfords and ribbons to wear in my hair.

Because I was accustomed to playing by myself, it was difficult for me to adjust to playing with others at school. So, I continued to play by myself. My cousin Lawrence, who was several grades ahead of me, went to the same school. While I would see and talk to him on occasion, we didn't get to play together because the playground was separated by grades.

My school life was pretty uneventful until I reached the third grade. There, I finally had a teacher named Ms. Williams, who seemed to take a real interest in me. One day after school, she took me to the local library and got me a library card. From that point on, books became my "best friend." Reading gave me all the things that I had been looking for: words, pride, self-accomplishment, self-esteem, and answers to many, many questions. I read all the time. When I wasn't doing chores, I was reading.

Looking back, my experiences at Mrs. Farley's were not all bad. After all, by the age of eight, I had learned to wash my clothes in a ringer-type washer and starch my own dresses by standing on a chair, boiling starch in a big pot. It was a constant challenge to keep the hot starch from burning my hands. I would carry a heavy laundry basket down the steps to the backyard, where I would hang the clothes on a droopy clothesline and hoist it up to the sun with a long board. Of course, I would hope it did not rain, but then again, people say, "It never rains in Southern California." I also learned how to iron my own dresses, make my bed, and clean the kitchen. I really didn't mind doing these chores because I knew that once I finished, I could go back to reading my books. There was, however, one chore that I simply hated to do—emptying the garbage. In those days, trash was burned in an incinerator. So, tin cans had to be put in separate containers from the garbage. The "can-man" would pick up the cans, and the "garbage man" would pick up the garbage. Separating the trash was no problem. However, the outside garbage bin, which had rats, roaches, and maggots crawling around everywhere, was a horrible sight. Just thinking of it even today still makes my flesh crawl. But, of course, like all adversity, doing these things made me stronger and more prepared for my future role as a homemaker.

Mrs. Farley was a very mean old lady who phys-ically abused me for years. My mom never knew about it until one Tuesday evening when I was in third grade. Just after school let out for the summer, Mom made one of her regular Tuesday evening visits. She usually stayed about an hour. We were sitting in the living room, discussing my class work when I noticed this strange look on her face. She leaned forward slightly and beckoned me to her. I came closer, knowing that she had noticed the large, red, swollen mark on my neck. "Verna, how did that get there?" she asked. I was reluctant to say anything; after all, I had never told my parents about Mrs. Farley's disciplinary tactics. Mrs. Farley had always convinced me I'd done something wrong. I feared that if my mom found out, she would be mad at me, too. Besides, most times, I was so glad to get home to my family on weekends, whatever abuse I had suffered during the week didn't seem important. Mom broke my silence with a more emphatic *"Verna, how did that get there?"* Finally, I looked up at her and simply said, "Mrs. Farley." I won't say she "snapped;" she was too much of a lady for that. I'll just say that she confronted Mrs. Farley. I remember Mrs. Farley saying, "I refuse to take care of a kid that I can't whip." During the confrontation, I went out on the front porch because I didn't want to witness what was happening.

It was a quiet night at the Farleys'. In fact, Mrs. Farley barely uttered a word. The next day, she began to help me pack all my belongings and then informed me that I would be going home for good. The next two days were very uneventful; it was as if we were all waiting for Friday to come, when I would leave the Farley household for the last time. When Friday finally arrived, I lay in bed, wondering if I had packed everything because I did not want to have to return for any reason. After bathing and eating a small breakfast, I thought I would get dressed and read until it was time for my parents to come get me.

At about four o'clock, I went to my usual sitting place on the front porch to begin my vigil of waiting and counting the cars for what would, hopefully, be the last time from the Farleys' porch. I was very quiet, but inside I was overjoyed, knowing that when I left, I would never return. The moment finally arrived when I saw my parents' car round the corner to the Farleys' house for the last time. While I was glad to be leaving, I also felt a pang of sadness as I waved my final farewell. Life was tough at Mrs. Farley's house, but it was the life that had been familiar to me for those seven years.

For me, the next day felt like the beginning of a new life. At home, everyday was now a special privilege. I would wake up every morning, thanking God for allowing me the opportunity that I had wished for for so long. My life at home was wonderful. It was summertime. I had friends close by. And, I could come and go as I pleased, without threat of physical abuse. Lord knows I took full advantage of my newfound freedom. On a good day, I would leave home as early as eight o'clock in the morning and wouldn't return until the streetlights came on. I spent most of my time playing with the kids next door and across the street. Sometimes I would venture out to other areas in the neighborhood. I also enjoyed playing in my own yard. It was peaceful. On some days, it was good just being alone in the serenity of my backyard. I always felt closer to God when I was outside in nature. I even tried my hand at a vegetable and flower garden in a corner of the backyard. I enjoyed the experience of planting a seed, nurturing it, and watching it grow. I began to enjoy life again. I could feel the wind kissing my face, not having any clue as to where it was coming from. I knew that it was the work of God. I saw mountains and other mysterious things and knew that there must be a God. Once again, life was good.

Although my mom allowed me the freedom to roam when she was home, mostly on the weekends, when she was working, it was a different matter. Because she did not want me to be left alone, she found another lady to baby-sit me. This baby-sitter, Ms. Leona, lived across the street. It seemed like it was going to be a wonderful, new experience compared to what I had been through at the Farleys'. Ms. Leona was one of the many interesting characters in our neighborhood. She also baby-sat another little girl named Trudy. Trudy and I had quite a lot in common. We were the same age, both the only child, and we liked a lot of the same things. Even though we were in the same grade, Trudy was a little more scholastically advanced than I was. This turned out to be a plus for me. There was nothing better than having a very smart best friend. Now that I had been introduced to reading, I felt that I could conquer anything. It was fun, yet challenging to compete with Trudy everyday. Our time together was short-lived, however, because she suddenly stopped coming to Ms. Leona's house. I wasn't sure why. All I knew was that I missed her.

Going to Ms. Leona's meant that when school started, I would be attending school in my neighborhood. I was excited about that because our community was full of interesting people. When Ms. Leona would send me down to the store, I walked slowly so that I wouldn't miss anything. One day as I skipped to the store, trying to remember what Ms. Leona told me to pick up, I passed what was considered the worst house on the block. Though I had passed it many times before, this time I decided to stop and walk into the front yard. As I did so, I suddenly became ill and passed out. An older couple who seemed to live like hermits were in the old, run-down house. The windows were covered with cardboard. I had heard that they used kerosene lamps for lighting because they had no electricity. I could see puffs of smoke billowing out through a vent at the top of the house from the wood-burning stove. The couple dressed in very old clothes and never talked to anybody. The kids in the neighborhood teased them.

To this day, I have no idea why I passed out in their yard. Someone in the house saw me lying on the ground and came out to see if I was all right. I could hear their voices, although they sounded very distant. When I came to, a lady from the house was wiping my face with something wet, and I could see a man whom I thought was her husband going to get Mrs. Leona. This was the first time anyone had known them to speak to others in the neighborhood. From that day forward, the little old couple always waved and greeted me every time I passed by. Eventually, they were forced to move because the authorities condemned their house.

My neighborhood had an international flavor. It was comprised of several ethnic groups, including Mexican, Black, Japanese, White, and Hawaiian families. All of the groups seemed to blend well together. I had friends from each of the diverse cultures, many of whom remain in my life today. I believe my early childhood experience of living in a culturally mixed neighborhood gave me the ability to mix well in any group. I learned to get along with everyone and to respect others for who they were from the inside out. Just as I had become more familiar with the neighborhood and its surroundings, the summer ended. It was time for me to enter the fourth grade.

My first day of fourth grade was a *horrifying* experience. That morning, my mother took me to the office of Mark Twain Elementary School, where I was assigned to a classroom. I remember feeling lonely and scared when my mother said good-bye because I was amongst strangers. The adjustment to being alone in a new school, meeting new students, and experiencing new teachers nearly sent me into a state of hysteria. Fortunately, the lady who escorted me to my new classroom was very nice. I was comforted by her friendliness and felt a little less nervous as I approached the classroom. When I entered it, I was surprised that the teacher and the students greeted me with friendly faces. After introducing me to the class, my new teacher, Ms. Gilliam, showed me to my desk. For the first time, I began to feel at ease. I felt that I could leave my past behind and create a new life in this improved environment.

The class was comprised of fourth and fifth graders. As a fourth grader, I took full advantage of learning from the more advanced fifth graders. This class was the steppingstone for my transformation from a timid girl to one who believed that the sky was the limit. I became a straight-A student. My parents were so proud of me that they took every opportunity to show off my report cards to our family and friends.

I became a sponge for knowledge. On some occasions when I went to the store with my parents, I would ask for a book instead of a toy. I spent more and more time in the library. I read everything, and I could spell anything. I became one of the top students and finally acquired the gift of self-esteem.

The summer between fourth and fifth grade was much like the previous summer. I spent most of my time becoming more familiar with my neighborhood and new friends from school.

I entered fifth grade with a ready-set-go attitude. I felt as though I could conquer anything. I eagerly tackled my studies. Once again, I became one of the top students in my class. My favorite subject was mathematics. I became an excellent speller, competing and winning spelling bees. I also developed award-winning penmanship.

At the end of each school year, we would receive a final report card, which would include the name of our teacher for the upcoming year. I had heard terrible things about one particular sixth-grade teacher named Mr. Wright. Everybody dreaded the thought of going to his class. When we received our report cards, everyone opened them with the seriousness that one would search a ballot for their favorite candidate. Throughout the class, you could hear expressions of excitement and dismay. I carefully opened mine with a sense of great anticipation, only to find that I had the teacher who had been described as a *demon*.

The summer after fifth grade was basically like all my other summers had been, except that I began to explore new areas of life.

My baby-sitter, Ms. Leona, moved away and a new family, the Brooms, moved into her house. My mother liked them because they seemed to be a very religious and well-rounded family. There were three boys and three girls, all of whom seemed to be no more than a year apart. The Brooms' home became my home away from home. In fact, I was there all day, everyday, until my parents got home.

As the summer drew to an end and it was time for back-to-school shopping, this time we were more selective about choosing articles of clothing that were more grown-up. My mom made a valiant effort to purchase everything I wanted in order to encourage me to do my best in school. I spent the night before school started organizing my outfits and planning the order in which I would wear them.

On the first day of school, I woke up early because I was excited. I got up in time to have breakfast with my parents before they left for work. I made sure that my clothes looked right and that my hair was styled to perfection for the sixth grade. As I took one last look in the mirror and gave myself a final approval, I grabbed my school supplies and headed across the street to walk to school with the Broom clan.

The first day in Mr. Wright's class was very different from my previous classroom experiences. Mr. Wright attempted to develop his students' abilities by making threats. If he believed a student had academic ability, he would push that student to the limit. Even though he was labeled as the meanest teacher at Mark Twain, he definitely made a positive impact on my life. In those days, corporal punishment was still allowed in schools. Mr. Wright always kept a paddle on his desk. If students answered questions incorrectly when called upon, he would swat them. I did everything I could to avoid being called on, but Mr. Wright seemed to love calling on me. For some reason, he thought I knew the answers to all of his questions. It was not that I didn't know most of the answers; I just didn't want to risk getting swatted if I happened not to know the answer. Occasionally I would give the wrong answer, and he would say, "Silverson, come here." He would demand that I hold out my hand and then would give me a rap across it. Those swats left me feeling as if part of my hand had come off on the paddle. Because I would take the punishment without crying, he referred to me as a *tough cookie*. After the swat, I couldn't wait to return to my seat so that I could place my hand against the desk. The cold metal seemed to offer me some quick relief.

While I was in the sixth grade, Mark Twain Elementary School developed its first athletic program. Mr. Wright thought I was smart enough and tough enough to be captain for our volleyball, baseball, and track teams. During the school year, I led all three teams to undefeated seasons. By the end of the year, I was amazed by my own accomplishments. The students and teachers knew me as both academically and athletically strong. I became very popular during that year. Needless to say, Mr. Wright's belief in my abilities inspired me to continue to do well.

As the year drew to a close, I thought about all that I had learned and wondered what, if anything, would be useful to me in the coming years. One thing was for certain—being an academically strong student was far more important and carried much more weight with people than just being a superior athlete.

I only got into one actual fight in school. The fact that I did not back down (and in some people's eyes, I actually won the fight) gave me the reputation of being a bad girl. This tended to keep negative encounters down to a precious few. It was kind of nice not having to worry about fighting and/or defending myself because I could just concentrate on getting good grades.

Being respected for my intelligence and my wit was a really cool thing. No one seemed able to surpass me in these two areas. In fact, my intelligence turned out to be my best asset. As a result, I was very focused on academic achievement. I was doing great in school and had little or no reason to think about anything bad or negative.

One day, a classmate's mother came to school to see a teacher. When I saw her, I was shocked by her appearance. This parent was dressed very shabbily and wore shoes that had the backs worn down. Her feet were dry and crusty, and she wore rollers in her hair that appeared to have been in for days. The dress she wore looked like a moo-moo that had grease spots and other residue splattered on the front. When the mother left, all the kids in the class laughed, including me. Children at that age can be very cruel and inconsiderate of the feelings of their classmates. And, of course, we teased and laughed at the boy, too. His feelings were quite hurt. In fact, he started to cry. I immediately felt great compassion for him and insisted that everyone stop laughing and ridiculing him. Upon reflecting on that event, I vowed never to put any children that I would have in a situation to be ridiculed in school by classmates for something that is not of their doing or under their control. I vowed never to show up, representing my family, without looking my very best. Looking your best was something that my mom had always drilled into my head, anyway. "Never leave home without looking decent; you never know whom you might meet," she would say. My mother said quite a few other things that I usually didn't remember until I was in a situation where I needed her wisdom. Mom did repeat the following pearls of wisdom that still remain with me today. They are, "There is no such thing as 'can't'," "If at first you don't succeed, try, try again," "If you don't accomplish your goal one way, turn around and approach it from a different angle," and lastly, "If you don't want to deal with the devil, stay off of his grounds."

During my last year at Mark Twain, my grandmother came to live with us. She was unquestionably one of the best grandmothers in the world. Grandma would sit in her rocking chair making quilts, while I sat close by catching all the pieces that she would discard. I used the scraps to make doll clothes. I would sit beside her wide-eyed, listening to her stories about our family history. By sitting at her side, I not only was entertained and educated by her stories, but I also learned to sew quite well. On one occasion, I made a skirt for myself completely by hand. When I wore that skirt to school the next day, I received lots of compliments. I responded proudly, "I made it." My grandma was willing to give what she had to me. I really learned a lot from her and her storytelling.

Picture taken in front of our house on 130th Street. From left to right: Aunt Stella, Uncle Jesse, Aunt Sarah, Roberta (my mom, Aunt Nellie, Aunt Sarah's Husband, Uncle Lumus, Gracie (my grandmother), Uncle Dave, Aunt Ethel, and Uncle Bob.

CHAPTER 5

Bad Decisions

hen the year ended, I was ready to graduate from Mark Twain. We spent time practicing the march, the speeches, and the songs. My mom took me shopping for the prettiest outfit. It was a most exciting time indeed. The thought of going on to the junior high left me feeling as if I were beginning a new and exciting life.

Graduation day was wonderful. My mom sat proudly in the audience as I walked across the stage to receive my diploma. I said good-bye to some of my classmates, some of whom I would probably never see again. Some of my elementary school classmates went on to Vanguard Junior High School with me.

I had another good summer (as all of my summers had been since I stopped going to Mrs. Farley's). I added new blocks to my normal neighborhood play territory and added new kids to my list of "hang-out" buddies. I even found a neighborhood that I didn't know existed just west of San Pedro Street. For years, I would pass by an area that consisted of a large field full of weeds and an old abandoned two-story house at the far end. During my last year in elementary school, there was quite a bit of construction going on in my neighborhood, much of it on the abandoned lot. The new junior high school which I would be attending was built there, as well as a new department store.

As the land was cleared for the department store, I discovered another community behind it. This community, while new to me, was actually not new at all. In fact, it was an old community that carried the nickname *Plumnelly*.

Why *Plumnelly*? As legend has it, it was called that because it was said to be "plum out of the city" and nearly "plum out of the world." Sounds corny, but that's what we were told as children.

I met lots of new and wonderful people in my new territory. In fact, many of them remain my friends today. Strangely enough, as close as Plumnelly was to my old stomping grounds, it was quite different from the neighborhoods to which I had grown accustomed. Oil fields were there, as well as a dairy, horse stables, farm animals in backyards, and many open fields. I thought this was about as close to country living as I would ever get. Many of the kids from Plumnelly were about my age, although there were quite a few older kids, too. Our neighborhood was divided into three groups. The oldest group was called "The Beat Boys." The group in my age bracket was called "Plumnelly." And the youngest group was referred to as the "Alley Tramps." We were not gangs. We all got along well and looked out for one another.

As I thought about going back to school at the end of the summer, I realized that going from elementary school to junior high school not only meant changing schools, but changing systems. I would now have to get used to having several teachers during the day, as opposed to one teacher all day. I would also have to become accustomed to new classmates. I looked forward to these and other new life challenges as I approached my teenage years.

The first day of the seventh grade was exciting. Everything was new: the school, books, chairs, and many of my friends, too! What I remember most about that day is that I met Bertie, another nervous, new seventh-grader, who would become my lifelong friend.

Bertie was very outgoing, friendly, and bright. She was an attractive girl with humongous lips and large, brown eyes. Bertie and I were both nervous and excited about starting our new adventure in junior high. I guess that is what helped form a bond between us. We found comfort in each other. It turned out that we had most of the same classes together. And, Bertie lived in my favorite new play territory—Plumnelly. We began doing many things together: playing, singing, studying, and competing for the best grades.

While Bertie was a good choice for a friend, I started making some poor decisions regarding picking new friends. I somehow got tied up with some friends who enjoyed clowning around. As a result, I ended up in the principal's office time and time again. Fortunately, my grades never slipped, so my mom did not know about my problems at school. Somehow, my friends seemed to escape punishment, including Bertie, but I never did. I seemed to care less about being the front-runner who headed straight into trouble. Eventually, I figured out that my new behavior and new friends were getting me nowhere fast. While I was having fun, I received low marks in citizenship. I knew that I could not continue down that road.

I began to pay more serious attention to school and my elective class, which was home economics. It included sewing. All those countless hours of sitting next to Grandma, learning to sew, really paid off in that class.

When it came to fashion, my grandma was a woman before her time. She inspired the fashion sense of her children, grandchildren, and great-grandchildren. Because of her teaching, I had a head start on everyone in my class. I even began to feel that sewing and fashion design were my true talents. I received an A-plus on my first project, which was a lady's three-piece suit. In fact, my project was showcased in the school's fashion show. As usual, my mom sat proudly in the audience while my fashions were displayed. Having her there at school events made me feel really good and boosted my overall morale. Mom's support allowed me to just about recover from the negative effect that Ms. Farley had had on my self-esteem. Mom recognized my potential in sewing. She even surprised me with my first sewing machine soon after the fashion show.

I tried very hard to stay focused and motivated about my newfound love for fashion, as well as my academic studies. I managed to remain on point throughout the seventh grade. The eighth grade was a totally different story, however. I completely lost focus and by midyear, I was expelled for the rest of the school year and sent to Willowbrook Junior High School. This school was used as a punishment to get me away from the group that I was hanging out with.

Going to Willowbrook was a lesson I would never forget. The school was located several blocks from my house at the corner of El Segundo Boulevard and Willowbrook Street. I rode to school with a neighbor who attended Centennial High School, which was near Willowbrook. Even though I made new friends there, I felt lost without my friends from the neighborhood. I especially missed Bertie, who remained at my old school. After school, I couldn't wait to get home to visit with her and other friends in Plumnelly. I did take up a casual friendship with some students from Willowbrook. Many of them loved to ditch class. At times, I ditched with them.

Needless to say, my grades suffered, and I barely made it through the eighth grade. I did make it, though. And, when eighth grade was over and the long awaited summer of '63 finally arrived, Plumnelly was my playground.

Boy, did we have fun playing baseball and all sorts of other games! We loved hanging out, making fun out of any- and everything. Neighborhood family parties went on throughout the summer. The parties were packed with kids from all over our neighborhood. Music was in the air. We all thought we were musically inclined. On occasion, we would breakout with jam sessions in the small garage at the Jackson's house, my favorite family of friends. The sound of music, piano, drums, as well as alto and tenor saxophones could be heard throughout the neighborhood.

Some of us who really thought we could sing formed a singing group called *The Four Aces*. We practiced at my house every chance we got if my mom allowed it. *The* Four Aces wrote music and played piano. Our voices blended beautifully in harmony. In order for the guys in the neighborhood not to be outdone, they formed their own little singing group called *The Romells*.

One member of that group was Theodore Young, who became my boyfriend. Theodore and I spent lots of time together during that summer. When summer was over, we still got together in the evenings and on weekends, mostly studying or just hanging out. Theodore went to Centennial High School.

When I started the ninth grade back at Vanguard Junior High School, I had an altogether new attitude about learning and vowed to stay out of trouble and never to be kicked out of school again. I began aggressively working toward improving my grades to the level that they were before.

I looked forward to the completion of junior high and graduation day. The school year passed pretty quickly. On graduation day, I was so thankful for the opportunity to receive my diploma. There were days that I thought it would never happen. As I think back on those days, I now realize that I not only learned a lot academically, but I also learned a lot about life in general and people in particular. After graduation, I looked forward to another fun-filled summer.

As usual, Bertie and I were still pretty tight, and Theodore was still my boyfriend. Life was good. But, that soon changed. For some reason, I started becoming ill frequently and was constantly fatigued. When my mom noticed my symptoms, she took me to the doctor. As she put it, "I'm too old of a cat to be fooled by a kitten." From that comment, I gathered that she suspected that I was pregnant. When the first pregnancy test came back negative, you can't imagine how relieved I was. However, the doctor wasn't convinced and suggested that I return in one month for a second test. Needless to say, that was the longest month of my young life. The symptoms continued the entire month. When I returned to the doctor for the second test, to my dismay, I found that I was definitely pregnant. Even though I acted shock, I think down deep inside, I really wasn't because I knew that I had been having sex with Theodore and that we hadn't been careful. From that point, my life changed forever. I was no longer the young schoolgirl getting in trouble for ditching class or the young lady concentrating on her studies. I was suddenly a woman, forced into making grown-up decisions long before I was ready. Many of the decisions I made to that point left me very confused. Because our carelessness resulted in pregnancy, Theodore and I were forced to make decisions that changed our lives in drastic ways.

My mom was adamant about us getting married. On the other hand, Theodore's mother was very much against it. Theodore was 17; I was only 15. We knew what we had done was wrong and were willing to do whatever it took to make amends. So, on August 22, 1964, Theodore and I were married in his mother's living room with a small group of our friends as witnesses. I became Verna Jean Young.

Because Theodore and I were both unemployed, we moved in with my parents. Theodore did not have much luck looking for employment. In 1964, jobs were scarce for most unskilled workers. Jobs that were available were frequently taken by more experienced adults. A seventeen-year-old, unskilled, inexperienced young person stood little chance of finding work. Unlike today when young people can find jobs at places such as fast food restaurants, movie theatres, and coffee shops, those types of jobs were not plentiful then.

One of the neighborhood mothers encouraged me to apply for welfare, so I did. Unlike today's welfare system where applicants go to the welfare office, social workers, or "workers," as they were called at that time, visited the homes of all welfare applicants. They inspected the homes like Nazi storm troopers to determine if an applicant was in dire enough need of "relief," or welfare. They did not want to see even the simplest items of convenience in your home, such as toasters, televisions, mixers, and radios. Even jewelry, no matter the worth, had to carefully be hidden from the intrusive eye of the worker to prevent the applicant from being disqualified.

On the day of my appointment, my worker showed up, ready to tear me down. She was armed with a questionnaire that contained very personal items. Some of the questions were so embarrassing to me that I refused to answer them. As a result, my welfare application was denied. Fortunately for us, our neighbors were very helpful. In fact, one of them assisted Theodore in landing his first job. Our neighbor, Mr. Willis, a construction worker, used his smooth-talking demeanor to convince the owner of the construction company to hire my new husband. We did not have a car, so Mr. Willis was also kind enough to pick up Theodore for work each day. The job was tenuous, because construction is a good-weather occupation. During the first three months, it seemed to rain constantly. And when it rained, Theodore didn't work. When he did work, however, he contributed to the household and even managed to save a little money toward our own place. While my husband was at work, I spent my day cleaning my parents' house and cooking to make it easy on Mom while we stayed there. I also read child psychology books, in preparation for our "new arrival."

With the help of my parents, we started looking for our own apartment after several months. We would all go out searching for affordable places to live. We were often disappointed, because what we could afford was generally not fit for habitation, at least, not for my family. And, some of the places we liked were reluctant to rent to such a young couple. Maybe we expected too much. But for us, living in an environment in which I could feel proud to entertain company was important. Even more important, as a young mother, I wanted to raise my child in a home free of roaches, rodents, and people of questionable character.

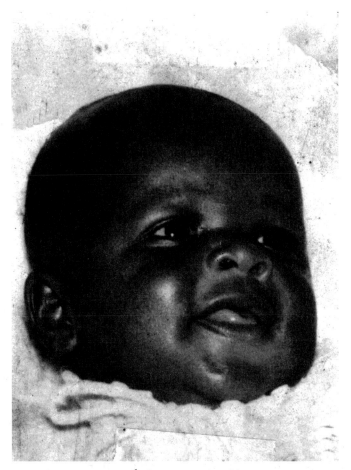

Andre 3 months old.

CHAPTER 6

Andre

During my pregnancy, I walked, read, and shopped a lot. I collected Blue Chip stamps and spent many hours selecting items that I could buy for my baby's layette. I was also a frequent visitor to a children's shop in Compton, called Hilda's Children's Shop. Hilda's had the most unique items that you could ever find for infants and children. I would carefully put together new outfits that I had purchased. As I shopped, I would often recount in my mind the mean things people said about me like, *Look at her. She's going to be a baby, taking care of baby; She's just a little fast thing that is going nowhere; or She ain't going to be nothing, and her baby ain't either.* Hearing these things obviously made me angry, but also strengthened my resolve that I was going to take good care of my baby.

When I got close to my due date, a pain like I'd never felt before sent everybody jumping and running to get me to L.A. County General Hospital, where my first child would be born. After I was admitted and prepped, I was taken to the labor room to await the wonderful moment. Meanwhile, absolutely no one could help me get through the pain I was feeling during labor. I just lay there, constantly preparing for the next pain to hit. The doctor checked on me occasionally to see how close I was to delivering. When I got to the point where I really just couldn't take the pain any longer, it seemed that the doctor appeared out of nowhere to give me the epidural.

Shortly after that, the most wonderful thing that could ever happen to a woman happened to me. Even though he seemed reluctant to come into this world, at 10:56 A.M., February 18, 1965, my son, Andre Romell Young, was born. He was a screaming, little, bald-headed, seven-pound bundle of joy. We chose Romell as his middle name after Theodore's singing group.

When the baby and I were released from the hospital, we went back to live with my parents for a few more months. Having a new baby meant a whole new way of living. Our days and nights included feedings, diaper changes, and formula preparations. Andre became my main concern. I thoroughly enjoyed being a mother. I read many books on baby care so that I would be fully equipped to be the best mother I could possibly be.

In June 1965, just four months after Andre was born, the Watts Riots broke out. This incident changed the world's perception of race relations in America and brought actual rioting in the streets to television. Those riots were believed by many historians to be the worst civil unrest in America since the Boston Tea Party or the Labor Riots of 1908.

I had never witnessed anything like it in my lifetime. I saw buildings burning, innocent white people being beaten, looting taking place, and complete destruction of property. It was a really scary, yet an exciting, time. Seeing National Guard tanks rolling through the neighborhood with armed military guards enforcing a ten o'clock curfew was quite invigorating from my sixteen-year-old perspective.

Most people look back on this historic event and find that several good things came about as a result. For instance, Black people in Los Angeles came together and worked with the authorities to prevent such violence in the future. They even parlayed the situation into opportunities for Black people.

After the event was behind us, Theodore and I proceeded to live our lives and continued to search for a decent place to live and to seek gainful employment. We soon learned that Theodore's stepfather, Richard, owned a house that he occasionally used as his "get away" on 135th Street. The house had two bedrooms and was completely furnished. He recognized the fact that we were having a hard time finding a place and was nice enough to let us rent the home for only $18.00 per week, not including utilities. Shortly after this, Theodore landed a job at a local laundry just a few blocks from the house. It seemed that things had turned around and were finally going our way. We started to feel like a real family.

Andre was a very friendly baby who would go to anyone. His four young uncles and two aunts, and what seemed like the entire neighborhood, loved to take turns holding him. When he was a few weeks old, like all parents, we were plagued with sleepless nights and early morning wake-ups. At first, we thought Andre only cried when he was hungry. Later, we found out that he was crying mostly because he wanted noise and people around him. *He didn't like the quiet.*

Andre loved hearing music, even when he was a baby. It seems that he was born with a love for music. When I look back on his life, I think he began to develop this love when he was only a few months old. That was when I first noticed the soothing effect that music had on him. When music was playing, he would lie content and look around as if he were searching for the direction from which the sound was coming. As long as he was full and dry, he would lie there listening to the music until he fell asleep.

Andre also loved to eat. So much so, that doctors recommended that we begin giving him baby food early. We initially fed him applesauce and rice cereal. He grew fast and became a big baby in a very short time. In the neighborhood, people teased me on a daily basis about Andre's size. "That boy is almost as big as you," they would say. Or, "You're going to need a wheelbarrow to carry that boy soon."

My grandmother felt Andre was far too heavy for a little person like me to tote around. She also realized that I didn't have much choice in carrying him because our money was tight. One day she surprised us with a brand-new stroller. In some ways, this became our only mode of transportation. After all, it was the only thing we owned with wheels, and everywhere we went, Andre went. Theodore had been raised with an old-fashioned attitude that women were not to work outside of the home. I guess that was okay with me. I just knew that I wanted to make sure that the house was perfect, if that was the way things were going to be. I spent my days cleaning, cooking, reading, and caring for our child. I carried out my job as a house-wife and mother meticulously.

By the time Andre reached nine months old, he was potty-trained and walking. I was amazed when he started pulling himself up on the furniture and was even more astounded when he let go and began walking. He never bothered to crawl. Perhaps he was too big to crawl, but all of a sudden, he was walking.

Andre seemed to do most things at an earlier than normal age. It seemed he learned to speak very clearly from the time he said his first words. People couldn't believe it when I told them how young he was.

Even back then, I suppose I should have known that Andre would be gifted with words. I can remember my mother teaching him poetry when he was a young child. She loved poetry and taught it to him when he was three years old. Of course, hip-hop was not even thought of back then, but I suppose God knew that Andre would be instrumental in creating an art form that combined his gift with words and his love for music.

Theodore and most of his friends worked the night shift at various jobs. His friends often stopped by after work to play cards and drink beer. One night while I was at home alone, I heard the side gate scraping against the house, as if it were being opened. Frightened, I stopped dead in my tracks and listened closely. I then heard footsteps coming up the walkway leading to the back steps. A man's silhouette appeared through the shade-covered window as the light from the kitchen reflected on it. I slowly eased off the sofa, walked across the room, carefully putting one foot in front the other, creeping so as not to make a sound. When I finally got to Andre's room, I slowly picked him up and went into the hallway to call my mother. I then went to my room, walking backwards all the way to make sure that the prowler would not surprise me.

Once back in my bedroom, I calmly waited for my mother or the police to come; it didn't matter who came first. I hadn't heard any glass break or the door creak, so I knew the prowler had not yet come into the house. Andre, who was asleep when I picked him up, by some miracle, did not awaken the whole time, even though I was squeezing him intensely. Time seemed to go by slowly. I fearfully waited, wishing that someone would come soon. I could hear the person testing the back doorknob, turning it back and forth, to see if it was unlocked. My heart was racing, but I didn't know what would happen if I tried to escape. All of a sudden, I heard the sound of a car door close, then another right after it. *Two people ...*, I thought. *Must be my mom and dad.* The two set of footsteps confirmed that it was definitely two people.

I rushed to the door, opened it, and to my relief, there stood my parents. I told them everything that had happened in what seemed like one single breath. The events occurred so quickly, but it seemed like an eternity. My dad went to the back door and grabbed the doorknob, expecting to pull the door open. Instead, the doorknob came off in his hand. My heart sank because I knew it was not my imagination. The loose doorknob was a clear indication that I had almost become a crime statistic.

After dad replaced the screws in the doorknob, my parents prepared to leave, assuring me that every-thing was going to be alright. I did not want them to go, at least not until Theodore got home. But they had to get up early for work in the morning. After checking around the house, dad felt that the danger was over. Besides, Theodore was due home very shortly.

Just as soon as they left, the mystery person returned. I could hear the footsteps again, approaching the back gate. Just then, I heard Theodore and his friends approaching the front door. I ran to him with Andre in my arms and frantically told him the story. They looked around, but didn't see a soul. Everyone left the kitchen except me. I calmed down and began preparing some of their favorite snacks. Suddenly, I heard the noise again! I ran out of the kitchen to alert Theodore that the intruder was still around.

He and his friends went to the back door, into the backyard, and jokingly called out, "Here kitty, kitty." Then Theodore immediately ran to the front door and threw it open. He chased the would-be intruder down the sidewalk, but was unable to catch him. After that terrible experience, he hired one of his friends to come over every evening, armed with a shotgun, to guard Andre and me while he was at work.

Wedding Day (1964). This is Andre's father; Theodore Young, and the Bride is me. Best Man, Kenneth Craig and Matron of Honor, Evelyn Finch. This picture was taken in Theodore's Mother's livingroom where the wedding took place.

CHAPTER 7

Theodore

While my husband was very protective of me if someone else tried to harm me, he was also high-strung, jealous, and abusive. If I went to the neighborhood store and stayed too long, he would beat me. If I engaged in what he considered a prolonged conversation with any of his male company, he would beat me. At that time, the only way I saw to keep from being beaten was to simply stay in my room until everyone left. I spent so much time out-of-sight when Theodore's friends were around, some of them probably didn't even know that he had a wife.

At one point, Theodore lost his job. I am not sure if it was due to tardiness, drugs, or what. I never found out the reason. All I know is that after he lost the job at the laundry, he began selling drugs. With drugs came a lot of unknown people. We constantly had to watch for the police and became very distrustful of strangers. When I saw a constant flow of strangers around the house, I wondered who they were. More than that, I wondered what had happened to my dream of a happy home. Sometimes I could look right outside my bedroom window and see suspicious-looking cars parked down the street. I feared that we would one day get busted. Deep down, I feared going to jail and having my baby taken away from me.

The stale odor of marijuana was so strong that not even daily cleaning could get rid of it. It was embedded in the furniture, drapes, bedding, and the walls—everywhere. Our house was not a happy home any more and had not been for some time. I really did not know what to do about it. I was a teenage mother who dropped out of high school with dreams of having a wonderful husband and taking care of my beautiful son. I only wanted to be the best wife and mother ever.

I had somehow ended up in another bad situation in my life, only this time, it was my fault. Sometimes, I would lay in bed at night, thinking back to my experiences at Mrs. Farley's. I would also think about all the wrong decisions that I had made, which put me in the situation that I faced today. I wondered, *Why me?*

One day, I decided I just couldn't take it anymore. After another of Theodore's brutal beatings, I packed up all of Andre's and my things, left that 135th Street house, and went back to stay with my parents. I wasn't concerned about Theodore coming after me because my dad did not play around, and Theodore knew it.

After moving back in with my folks, I tried to get my life together. I ran across an advertisement announcing the Neighborhood Youth Corp (NYC). NYC was one of the many government social programs that emerged after the Watts Riots. NYC was created for youth, ages sixteen to twenty-one—people who had either dropped out of school or were simply having a hard time finding jobs. Youth under twenty-one years old needed their parents' written consent in order to work. Because I was married and underage, I needed my husband's, rather than my parents', consent. There was no way in hell that I would risk getting Theodore's consent. *I didn't need anything from him anymore*, so I thought. Therefore, I decided to forge his signature. This was my first act in asserting my independence, and it felt good. I signed his name, turned in the consent form, and was immediately enrolled in the program that would change my life.

After enrollment and a brief orientation, my group was prepared to work for various companies that were affiliated with the NYC program. I was fortunate enough to be hired by the NYC staff, which allowed me to work in the headquarters. My first position was as an office clerk, working side by side with my supervisor, Norida Comminey, who was known in the office as Chickee. Chickee and I got along quite well and developed a pretty close relationship. I was her "right hand" at work and a friend away from the workplace.

I really liked my job and generally enjoyed working. I especially enjoyed going out to assigned companies to collect time cards, helping to solve any problems employers may have had with NYC employees, and delivering checks on payday.

Theodore's mother agreed to watch Andre while I was at work. During this time, Theodore tried to get me to come back to him. In a matter of weeks, he sweet-talked me into coming back home, with promises never to be violent again. I went back to 135th Street to live with him, hoping to keep my family together. We got off to a good start. Even though he was uncomfortable with the fact that I had a job, I convinced him that we needed my income. During the first few months, Theodore didn't lay a hand on me. However, after a few months, during which time I became pregnant, the abuse started again. This time, I wasn't at all hesitant about leaving.

I had friends like Bertie with whom I had maintained a long-distance friendship while she was at school. And, I had Chickee to talk to for moral support. I left Theodore once again and spent the rest of my pregnancy living with my parents. I worked all the way up until I was eight months pregnant. In fact, my co-workers were all afraid that I was going to give birth right there in the office.

On August 18, 1966, I gave birth to my second son, another potential star, Jerome La Vonte Young. Andre loved his baby brother from the beginning. He liked to call him "Bubby." After the baby was born, I allowed Theodore to convince me to move back home again. I really wanted my family to be together; that was all that seemed to matter.

My friends were opposed to my decision. They said that I was doing so well on my own. I couldn't get them to realize how much I really just wanted to have a family. My parents and grandparents had families. That's what I wanted, too! So, I returned home, only to discover that Theodore had not paid some of the bills, so the utilities had been turned off. Regardless, I felt where I belonged was with my family.

Once again, we got off to a pretty good start with the new baby. I returned to work and, although Theodore was not working, there were no signs of drug activity around our home. After I had been home for about two months, I got up one morning to begin my normal routine of feeding the boys and getting dressed for work. I fixed Jerome's bottle, then returned to our bedroom to change his diaper. When I pulled back his blanket, I knew instantly something was terribly wrong. I turned him over and saw a blood-spotted sheet. The blood had come from his nose. Hysterical, I grabbed him. His head dangled like a loosely filled rag doll. When I realized that he wasn't moving, I screamed at the top of my lungs. Theodore sprang out of bed and took Jerome from my arms. He administered CPR repeatedly in an effort to revive him. Because we did not have a telephone, I ran barefooted down to the corner telephone booth to call my mother. Within minutes, she arrived to find me crying hysterically. Theodore was clinging to Jerome, saying repeatedly, "He's going to be alright." We quickly jumped in my mom's car and rushed to Bon Air Hospital, where Jerome was pronounced dead on arrival.

The cause of death was intestinal pneumonia. I wondered how that could be, because just a few days before this occurred, I had taken him to the clinic, and the doctor said that he was a perfectly healthy baby. My whole world went numb when my baby died. I had seen this happen to other people, but I couldn't believe it was happening to me. Despite my numbness, I had the responsibility of preparing for a funeral. There were many decisions to be made, and I was so unprepared to make them.

I had never before seen such a small casket. Before I knew it, the whole thing was over, and it was time to go home *without* Jerome. When I got home, everything seemed so different. Even though Jerome's life was so short, his absence had already left a great emptiness in our home. Andre really missed him. I could tell because he reverted back to asking for the bottle and occasionally wetting his pants. He would look in the crib and call out, "Bubby! Bubby!" For months afterwards, I could hear a baby crying in the distance.

One summer afternoon, the guys from the neighborhood gathered outside the house to hang out and shoot the breeze, as they did on occasion. I was inside doing my usual cleaning and caring for Andre. Theodore came rushing in the house, saying that there had been a fight between two of the neighborhood guys. One of them, Johnnie Doyle, had a reputation for being very headstrong and destructive. The other guy, Joe Brown, was basically a good guy, at least in my opinion.

Well, after Joe seemed to have given Johnnie all that he could handle, Johnnie had angrily left the scene, threatening to come back and kill him. As I looked out the window, I could see Joe pacing back and forth while the other guys continued their normal activities. Everyone was wondering whether or not Johnnie would return. After a while, I decided Johnnie was probably just bluffing and went back to my chores and Andre. I walked Andre down the back steps to the backyard, where I prepared to hang clothes on the line. Just as I went back into the house to get my basket of clothes, I heard the distinct sound of a car with loud headers. I knew it had to be Johnnie, because his car was the only one that made that sound.

I immediately went back out into the yard to bring Andre inside.

After putting Andre in his room, I ran to the front door to see where Theodore was. Right before I got there, I heard a loud blast that echoed fiercely in my ears. I opened the door to see Johnnie speeding away. I didn't see Theodore. I thought to myself, *Theodore, where are you?* I didn't holler out; I was trying to remain calm. I then noticed Joe, lying against the curb. For a few minutes—which seemed like forever—no one said a word. Like a photo, everyone seemed stuck in time. Then, two of the guys dragged Joe to a car and rushed him to the hospital, possibly the same one where my precious Jerome had died. I didn't recognize them because of my shock. *Oh, God, not again*, I thought.

I finally spotted Theodore standing in the crowd with several of his friends. Within hours, we got the news that Joe had died. I can remember hearing the song "Bumpin' on Sunset," by Wes Montgomery, playing on the radio as if it were a tribute to Joe. For years afterwards, even though I loved that song, I hated to hear it because it always made me believe that something bad was about to happen.

Traumatized by the loss of his son and his friend, Theodore seemed to always be on edge. I tried hard to keep him happy. I was especially careful not to do anything that would cause him to be abusive.

One day, three of my girlfriends came over to ask me to go to a party. They knew that I needed Theodore's permission. I was reluctant for them to ask for fear he would get angry. One of my girlfriends said, "The hell with this; I'll ask him." Surprisingly, Theodore agreed. I was still a little reluctant to go, despite the fact that Theodore had consented to it and even encouraged me to go. I should have known that it was really too good to be true. I found it really hard to believe that Theodore had finally realized that I worked hard at being a good wife and that I needed some time to hang out with my girlfriends.

I smelled trouble. Yet, I was so excited about going out with my friends that I didn't think anymore about what his motives might have been. I had not been out with my friends in quite some time (or even with Theodore, for that matter). A guy named Tony, who was one of my girlfriend's boyfriend, escorted us. He was not present when Theodore gave me permission to go. I was so excited about going that I didn't give that fact a second thought. My mother agreed to watch Andre. The stage was set for a wonderful evening.

The party was great, in spite of the fact that I couldn't do any of the new dances. I was 18 years old and already out of style. I had fun learning the latest steps, even though the dances would probably be different before I got to come out again. A repeat performance was the last thing on my mind; I was just having a wonderful time. After the party, Tony dropped everybody off. When he got to my house, he decided that he wanted to talk with Theodore about something. They knew each other quite well, so this was not something I gave much thought about. We picked up Andre from my mom's house and headed to my home.

When we got there, Theodore was lying on the sofa, obviously under the influence of drugs, alcohol, or both. He struggled in vain to get up, although he did manage to raise his head up long enough to say, "I ought to blow your brains out." At that very moment, I realized that I shouldn't have gone. I should have known that this was all too good to be true. I went into the bedroom, preparing for the beating that I knew was coming.

As I heard Tony and Theodore talking, I prayed that Tony would not leave, or that he would at least talk Theodore out of beating me. After I laid Andre down, I went to the closet to hang up his coat. That was when I noticed that the shotgun Theodore kept in the corner of the closet was missing. I immediately put Andre's coat back on, put some more things in a bag, and asked Tony to take me back to my mother's house. Theodore was drunk or high and really could not do much harm to Tony and probably wouldn't try. Tony gave me his keys and told me to go to his car. He knew that I would be in danger if I stayed. He remained behind to talk to Theodore until he knew I was safely in the car. He ended the conversation, came out to the car, and drove me to my parents' house. Before he left, Tony warned me not to go back to Theodore. Andre and I had a peaceful night, but the next day, it all was a living hell.

I am sure that after Theodore awoke from his intoxicated state, he realized that he had gotten cheated out of the whipping he had planned to give me the night before. That morning, he started calling with threats to beat me if I didn't come home. When I stopped answering the phone, he threatened whoever answered—my mom, dad, or grandmother. I was determined to be strong. This time, I was not going back. My dream of a wonderful family, being a good wife, and having a loving husband disappeared at that moment. Theodore began stalking me. Any place he thought I might be, he showed up. I was afraid to go anywhere. When I did go out, I was constantly looking over my shoulder. As much as I hated to, I quit my job because I knew that Theodore would eventually show up there. I did not want to run the risk of being there when he did.

One night after lots of persuasion from friends, I decided to venture out from my parents' home. Bertie and her boyfriend Donald stopped by, and we decided to go for a ride. That's what people did in the sixties when there was nothing else to do. Since Andre was with my mom, I was in no rush to get home. I got into the backseat of Donald's car, and off we went. Donald had a record player in his car, like most cool guys who had cars. He just happened to put on "Bumpin' on Sunset." I told him, "Donald, I'm sorry, but that's my bad luck song. Every time I've heard it, something bad happens." I asked him to take it off. He just laughed and said, "Aw, Verna! Nothing's going to happen to you. You're with me."

No sooner than we reached the end of the block, we noticed a car speeding straight toward us. The headlights from the approaching car were so bright, I could hardly see. Before we knew what was happening, my car door flew open, and Theodore pulled me out, forcing me into the front seat of his car. Rabbit, one of our friends, was also sitting in the front passenger seat. Theodore jumped in behind me. There I was, sandwiched in between the two of them. Theodore looked at me with pure hatred in his eyes and declared, "You will never leave me again."

At that moment, my entire life flashed in front of me. All I could think about was how to keep this from happening. There was no way I was going to go home with him. There was no way I would take a beating from him tonight or ever again. I had to think fast. When Theodore's car came to a stop at the red light at the intersection of Main and Manchester Street, I noticed that Rabbit seemed to be in deep thought. Perhaps he knew, like I knew, that Theodore would beat me if he ever got me home. Rabbit nervously pushed his seat back as far as he possibly could, giving me the room I needed to jump, if I so chose.

At that moment, I reached across Rabbit, grabbed the door handle, opened the car door, and slid across his lap in what seemed to be all one motion. Once out of the car, I noticed that an auto parts store called Sopp's was open and ran inside. Theodore swirled his car into the parking lot, coming dangerously close to hitting me. His car was now between the store and me. I quickly ran around the car and into the store. The security officer on duty had seen me run frantically into the store and protectively drew his gun.

Determined to catch me, Theodore ran into the store behind me. At that point, it seemed as if he were driven by just foolish, blind rage. When the officer ordered him to stop, Theodore challenged him. The officer begged him not to force him to shoot. I stood, shaking with nervous confusion. I wanted him to leave me alone. At the same time, I didn't want to see him hurt. Theodore finally calmed down, and the officer called the police.

I cried because I knew through all of this, Theodore would eventually get me where he wanted me—home and alone. I felt sure that I would get a severe beating and possibly be killed. In those days, police rarely did anything when they were called for domestic disputes. When the police arrived, they decided that it was best for me to go back to my parents' house. They took me there, which was my shelter and refuge. There was no way that Theodore would show up at my parents' house, acting stupid. But everywhere else I went, he was there, stalking me. There seemed to be no escaping from him. Time and time again, I narrowly escaped running into him. To avoid these constant close calls, I opted to stay at home. In fact, my parents' home became my little prison. Theodore had made so many threats against my family and me that I wasn't even sure if staying home was safe, either.

When I did leave home, I was afraid to go alone. I didn't think he was that crazy, but I wasn't sure. My girlfriends, Bertie and Bobbie, often came by to comfort me. They would talk about the places that they had been and the fun that they had had. I was still young and wanted to go out and have fun like they did. But, my fear that Theodore would show up was always stronger than my desire to go anywhere.

One day, I got word that the house on 135th Street where I had lived had been raided and that Theodore had been arrested. The feeling I had that day was indescribable. I felt like how I imagined the slaves must have felt when they were told they were free. His arrest was the talk of the neighborhood. The police had actually secured evidence collected during a series of stakeouts. Several other people were booked and jailed, in addition to Theodore, who was the big fish. He was charged with possession with intent to sell and distribute illegal drugs.

After his arrest, I let things cool down for a few days. Then I went to the house to pick up several items that belonged to Andre and me. When I got there, the house didn't look anything like it did when I left it. The police had bashed in both the front and back doors. The cabinets and drawers were emptied, with the contents strewn all over the floor, and the sofa, chairs, and mattresses were slashed. They had even rolled the carpet up to the middle of the floor.

As I hurriedly gathered our belongings, I couldn't help but think how fortunate I had been that I wasn't there when it all went down. I felt as though I was finally making some worthwhile and constructive decisions in life.

As I took one last glimpse at the shambles, visions of the misery I had suffered in that house rushed through my mind. I pondered my life with Theodore, the dreams I had when we first came here, and the thoughts I had had of a wonderful life with a wonderful man. There were some good times. I couldn't help but think that I was the reason he acted so satanically at times. After all, we were just children when we were suddenly forced to make adult decisions, and Theodore was suddenly forced into manhood. I suppose that is something that happens to lots of teens. Some make it through; some don't. Theodore didn't.

Andre at the age of three.

CHAPTER 8

Party Time

had plenty of time to ponder the *whys* and *what ifs* about Theodore and me. But first, it was *party time*. I decided not to take any time to deal with my sadness. I immediately got into the street life instead. I went wild! Without having to worry about the threat of Theodore, I was likely to party all the time, at least for the time being.

I started my new life by running the streets with Bertie and Bobbie, two lifelong friends who had stuck with me through everything. We always had a good time together and always had each other's backs. We were all about eighteen. Bobbie had just returned home from the Job Corps, and

Bertie was preparing for her final semester of high school. But she quit school rather than finish. Unlike me, it wasn't that she was pregnant; she just didn't want to go.

We were out cruising one evening and stopped at the corner of Central Avenue and 87th Street when two cars filled with guys came around the corner. Bertie yelled out to them, as if she knew one of them from school. They stopped, pulled over, and we all talked for a while. Bobbie and Bertie exchanged telephone numbers with some of them. Not me. I was still enjoying my freedom. Within a few weeks, Bertie and Bobbie were both dating two of the guys we met that night.

One day, Andre and I were invited to a beach party with a group of our new friends. I was so excited about going because I had never been to a beach party before. I packed Andre's bag, and we went along for what turned out to be an unusually wild experience. I had never been around such crazy-acting people before. It was so much fun. At this party, I met Curtis Crayon. Curtis was the brother of Bertie's new boyfriend, Donald. He was one of the funniest people I had ever met. He seemed to thrive on getting a laugh or two. Because I had Andre with me, I couldn't party too much. I enjoyed the treat of cuddling Andre, talking to Curtis, and watching everyone having fun. Curtis was a nice guy. When I left, I told him how much I had enjoyed meeting him.

Everyone hung out in a neighborhood near Manchester at Central Avenue. All of our new friends lived in that area. Bobbie was dating a guy named Dino, who lived in the area of Manchester at Main. I would constantly leave Andre with my mother so that I could party with my new friends. She knew what I had been through with Theodore, and I guess she thought that I needed to have some fun, which I didn't mind at all. I had left Andre with my parents so much that people started thinking he was their child.

On many nights, the whole group of us would drink alcohol until we were drunk senseless. Bertie, Bobbie, and I would go to the party any way we could so that we could drink. If no one was available to pick us up, we would catch the bus, walk, or occasionally get bold enough to hitchhike in order to be with our friends.

What seemed to be a good time rapidly took its toll. At times when I partied and drank, I thought I heard a baby crying in the distance. I knew it wasn't Andre; it was just my mind playing tricks on me. The unpleasant memories of my battered and abusive life seemed to be fading in the distance. Although I didn't know it at the time, in retrospect, I realize that all the partying I was doing only gave me temporary relief from the miseries that I had suffered.

The party group seemed to get bigger and bigger. And, a relationship between Curtis and me began to blossom. He made me laugh, something that had been missing in my life. He also indulged in the fast life of drinking and partying.

Our partying included going to clubs. Even though my girlfriends and I were not of age to get into the clubs, a little make-up, fancy hairstyles, and the right clothing got us in without a problem. When we got inside, we saw everyone we knew from our new group of friends. It was great fun. The house of our friend Georgia would sometimes be the last stop for the evening. We would sleep over, and then wake up, ready to party all over again.

After a few months of this routine, I began to recognize the truth in the old saying, "Misery loves company." People would chip in a dollar on a drink or however much they felt they needed to get high on. We shared everything to the very last drop. Looking back, it seems ironic that we were able to find money and resources to support our wrong doings, yet we refused to help each other in positive ways. Some of my friends indulged in different types of drugs. Although I didn't do some of those things, I was around them enough to recognize the symptoms of each. There was so much addiction going on that people actually quit jobs just to hang out with us. They seemed to be unable to resist the temptations that this fast life offered.

Eventually, I came to the conclusion that I wasn't accomplishing much with the life I was leading. As I started taking a closer look at the situation, I saw friends that were scarred from falls they had taken while drunk, including me. Some of the wounds wouldn't heal easily because of the overuse of alcohol.

One night, after coming from a club where Bertie and I had a few too many drinks, I ended up back at Georgia's house, where we often hung out. One male friend was there who was always trying to talk to me. I didn't want to be bothered with him then or any other time, for that matter. Yet, he continued to try to talk with me, even though I was pretty rude to him. Since I was wasted, I don't remember this, but everyone present said that I finally exploded at him. I started viciously swinging my fist at him in an attempt to make him leave me alone. In his effort to stop me from hitting him, he accidentally knocked me backwards. I fell like a limp rag doll. I happened to be standing in front of the kitchen back door that had a sash window. So when I fell backwards, my head crashed through the window. My friends pulled me back through it. The scary part about this incident is that I didn't remember anything after throwing the punches. The next day, everyone who had witnessed this bizarre display told me how lucky I had been.

I could not comprehend what they were talking about until they recapped the whole story. I escaped this ordeal without a scratch, again.

This was the second time in my life that I was aware of how the Lord had intervened to save me from harm: first, that night at the auto parts store, and second, the night when I fell though the window without receiving a scrape. Like the poem, "Footprints in the Sand," this is one time where there was only one set of footprints because I believe the Lord had carried me. An old saying states that God takes care of babies and fools. Given all the foolish things I had done at such a young age, I probably fit into both categories.

Soon after that incident, I finally came to my senses and walked away from the party scene forever. I had been on the verge of quitting. It just took this close call with death for me to actually walk away. For months, I was haunted by thoughts of seeing Andre cry each time I left to go out partying. What would happen to him if something happened to me? I was all he had besides his wonderful grandparents, who were always there for both of us. I was just a child myself. With Andre and me, it was as though my parents had two children.

I started staying home and reclaiming my role as Andre's mother. My decision to leave the party scene seemed to be infectious. Curtis soon left the group behind, as did my best friends, Bertie and Bobbie. My life was beginning to make sense. A few of us had managed to escape a lifestyle that was moving nowhere fast.

With our terrible past behind us, we all started in a more positive direction. I filed for divorce and went to the Neighborhood Youth Corp (NYC) to get my job back. Unfortunately, my former position had become automated. In fact, there had been many other changes in NYC procedures that resulted in the loss of traditional jobs.

I was offered a position at the Compton Police Department, which was an NYC-designated company. I felt the Lord working in my life again. I began working in the Traffic Division. It was my job to pinpoint accidents on a huge map of the city, as well as file and update the status of tickets. Because Curtis was mechanically inclined, he landed a part-time position repairing motorcycles at the shop where his dad also worked. Bertie got a job through the Neighborhood Youth Corp working in the Economic Youth Opportunity Agency (E.Y.O.A.) Office. E.Y.O.A., like NYC, was another state-funded agency that assisted youth in finding employment. After Bertie started working at E.Y.O.A., she helped me find a job there. My office was one floor above hers.

Bertie and I started saving our money in contemplation of getting an apartment together. At almost nineteen, we felt that we were too grown to live with our parents. After all, we had seen so much from our days on the street, we found living with our parents difficult. Bertie had become a very close friend. We did most everything together. We were even dating brothers.

As soon as Bertie and I had finally saved up enough money, we started our search for an apartment. Our goal was to find a nice place in a good area that was safe and suitable for two young ladies and a small child. We were rejected a few times because of our ages, but we were finally able to find an apartment that we were truly proud of. Our new home was located near the corner of Vermont and Gage Avenue, which was convenient to everything we needed. We were directly across the street from a Safeway market. A bus stop and shopping center were also within walking distance. The bus dropped us in front of the building where we worked. Bobbie and a few other friends also moved within walking distance.

My greatest challenge was childcare. We didn't have a car to transport Andre back and forth to the baby-sitter who lived across the street from my mom. But my mom, being her usual supportive self, kept Andre during the workweek. She would take him to and from the baby-sitter and see to all his other needs. On weekends, my parents would drop him off at my apartment to spend the weekends with me. I couldn't help but feel guilty about being away from him so much. At the time, there wasn't much that I could do about it. My parents knew it; even at his young age, Andre seemed to understand, also. This was almost like a repeat of my early childhood, except I knew that he was in good hands. Thank God for my mom. I was on a mission to better myself. Because mom understood that, she was willing to help whenever she could, and my dad was always supportive in her efforts. During the time that I was out in the streets, she did a lot of praying and crying. It paid off. God must have heard her prayers, and the life insurance policy she had for me was still in good standing.

Not long after Bertie and I had completely settled in our apartment, I found out that I was once again pregnant. Curtis handled the news quite well. He was very adamant about seeing to my well-being and helped by giving me money for groceries and other essentials. He would stop by daily on his way from work and would sometimes stay overnight. We didn't discuss marriage. Maybe he knew I just wasn't interested in marriage, or maybe the thought never entered his mind.

Curtis' brother, Donald, would occasionally visit with Bertie. More often than not, all they did was hang out and drink, which was something I no longer wanted any part of. I didn't have a problem with them drinking. Until rent money was due, I never said anything. Finally, Bertie missed a couple of months rent and decided to move back home. Curtis and I thought that Bertie's move was for the best because it allowed me to have the apartment all to myself. Curtis agreed to help me financially.

The day after I had cleaned the apartment from top to bottom, Curtis and I went to the movies. When we returned, we noticed a light on, even though I was pretty sure that I hadn't left one on. As we approached the door, we heard heavy laughter coming from inside. We also noticed that the screen was not quite attached to the window. When we opened the door, we saw Bertie and Donald sitting on the floor, smoking and drinking Old English 800 brew. The house reeked of a strong brew scent unlike the clean smell when I had left. Bertie no longer had a key, but had climbed in the window. I was so mad that I could have screamed. Even though Bertie had moved back home, she thought it was alright to come back to hang out at the apartment, rent-free.

I didn't want to lose our friendship, so I decided to give up the apartment and return to my parents' house. I hated to leave such a nice, well-kept place with all of its conveniences, but I felt that this was the best thing to do. Not only that, I had become overwhelmed with guilt about only seeing Andre on the weekends. Moving back home was the best thing for Andre and me. And, with a new baby soon to arrive, I could get help from my parents until I was able to get back on my feet. As always, they were there to support me.

My relationship with Curtis continued to blossom. He came and called often. One day, he called me to say that he was in jail. He explained that his sister, Elaine, had asked him to come over to her apartment to do a favor. When he arrived, he found a note on the door, instructing him to go downstairs and wait for her at a neighbor's apartment. When he got down there, Curtis found himself in the midst of a raid. The neighbor was dealing drugs. Everyone in the house went to jail. This was nothing but a case of being in the wrong place at the right time. Curtis wound up being locked up for ninety days. I visited him at the county jail from time to time.

I think that my sudden change from being hardly noticeable to being extra large made my supervisor a little nervous. So, I was forced to take leave from my job two months before my baby was due. On my last day at work, the people in the office showered me with so many baby gifts that Bertie and I could barely make it home. A few days later, I woke up in the morning feeling kind of strange. I had planned to visit Curtis and then go to L.A. General Hospital. As I was preparing to leave, Bertie dropped by on her way to work. I dressed Andre and took him across the street to the baby-sitter and then headed to the bus stop with Bertie. Bertie's stop came first. I went on to my second bus alone.

When I arrived at the jail, I filled out a visit form and stood in line to submit it. While doing that, I felt a slight pain. I asked the lady behind me to save my place in line while I went to get a drink of water. When I got back, there were only a few people in front of me. I had only been back in line a few minutes when I felt another pain. Determined to follow through with my plans for seeing Curtis before going to the hospital, I got out of line, walked until the pain subsided, and returned. Now there was only one person ahead of me. I managed to turn my visitor's slip in and sit down for a hot second before a stronger pain hit me. At that point, I knew that it was time to go.

I headed over to the administration building to call a taxi; however, my labor pains were so strong that I couldn't even talk. Because they came too fast to bear, I went to lie down on a bench inside the building. A lady who walked by and saw me lying there stopped to ask if I was all right. When she realized that I was in labor, she frantically ran for help. She came back to tell me that she was having difficulty getting anyone's attention because everyone was busy. Once again, she ran frantically to see if she could find help. This time, she returned with her brother-in-law. He got me up and hurriedly, but carefully, walked me outside the building towards the parking lot. As we walked, I became weak at the knees and slumped to the ground. In a desperate attempt to keep me from falling, the man scooped me up in his arms and ran to the car. After carefully placing me in the backseat, he sat next to me, trying his best to comfort me as the lady drove hastily toward the hospital. At one point, she made a wrong turn, which led us into an area of warehouses and trucking yards. Every time I would moan, she got more and more nervous. Within minutes, we were back on the main street. As luck would have it, a police officer was traveling in the opposite direction. The lady jumped out of her car, flagged down the officer, and told him what the problem was. She then jumped back in the car and followed the police car, with sirens blaring, all the way to the hospital.

When we arrived, the lady's brother-in-law ran into the emergency room, carrying me in his arms. After I was admitted, a red blanket was thrown over me. I was whisked up to the delivery room, bypassing all of the bleeding, moaning, and desperately ill patients in the emergency waiting room. Before the lady and her brother-in-law could even leave the hospital, I gave birth to a baby boy. Because it was an emergency, no one stopped to take the names of the persons who brought me to the hospital. To this day, I do not know who those people were.

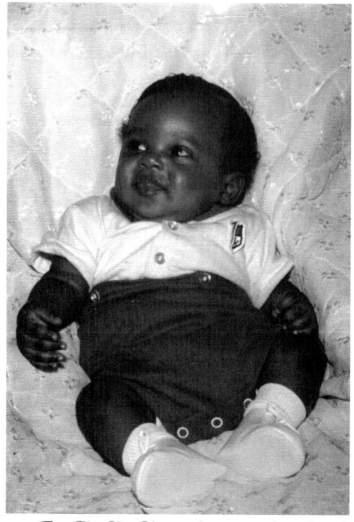

Tyree Du Sean Crayon (3 months old) son #3.

CHAPTER 9

Birth of Tyree & Marriage to Curtis

yree Du Sean Crayon was born March 19, 1968. He was two months premature and weighed only four pounds eleven ounces. When I was released from the hospital, I was unable to take Tyree home until he weighed five pounds. My father picked me up from the hospital on his lunch break and brought me back to the place where he worked, where I would wait until he got off. As I sat in the car, I wasn't feeling very well at all. When I got home, all I wanted to do was lie down. In addition to hurting physically, I felt depressed about not being able to bring Tyree home. After I had finally managed to get a few hours of sleep, an excruciating abdominal pain suddenly woke me up. I got my mom to rush me back to the hospital. The car would not start so we had to call Uncle Dave, my mom's big brother, who lived close by.

Although I saw Uncle Dave often, he sure was a sight for sore eyes that night, given all the pain I was in. I felt every bump, every turn, and every stop; I felt them all, right in the pit of my stomach as we rode. I felt my body temperature rising rapidly. The pain was actually worse than the labor pains. I was thinking all sorts of wild thoughts. *Was there still another baby in me? Did they release me too soon?* I even thought I was going to die!

When we finally arrived at the hospital, my temperature was 104 degrees. I was rushed into the examination room. I could hear the nurse trying to calm down my crying mother. The examination revealed that the doctors had failed to remove the afterbirth when they delivered Tyree. They rushed me into surgery to repair the problem. Relieved from the pain, I was finally able to go to sleep. After several days of recovery, I felt like I had been given a new lease on life. I did not like being in the hospital room by myself and was quite eager to go home. I had been told that it would still be a few more days before I could take Tyree home. I truly hated the thought of leaving my baby there again.

At home, Andre was waiting anxiously to meet his new brother. My mom had already explained to

him that he would soon be able to greet his new playmate. Waiting to pick up baby Tyree only took a few
days, but it seemed to take a lifetime for the day to
arrive when we could bring him home from the
hospital. He was quite small, but he seemed to be very
strong. We felt confident that he would be alright.

When we got home, Andre thought his new
playmate would be able to play immediately. He was
so excited that he ran to get his favorite ball and
prepared to toss it to Tyree. I explained to him that the
baby had to get a little bit bigger before he could play.
He was a tad bit disappointed at first. I remedied that
by giving him "big brother duties," such as assisting
with changing diapers, feedings, and occasionally
holding him. I was fortunate because the hospital staff
had already gotten Tyree on a regular sleeping and
eating schedule.

As I cared for this new little boy, the memory of
Jerome's death caused me to focus on whether Tyree
was still breathing. After a while, I became comfortable that he was healthy, so I stopped my constant
checking. Yet, after losing a baby, I don't think I ever
became completely at ease with my child's health.

When Tyree was about two months old, I
prepared to go back to work. Andre's sitter agreed to
keep both boys. All I needed to do was to find a job.
Bertie, who was consistently checking on me to make
sure all was well, came by to let me know that she had
gotten a new job at Pacific Telephone and Telegraph

Company. I wanted to work there, also. She obtained the job through the E.Y.O.A., but that program had ended. I went directly to the Pacific Telephone and Telegraph Company's employment office, filled out an application, and took the employment test.

I passed the test with flying colors and was hired as a compilation clerk. I was responsible for associating bills with all the necessary forms and preparing them for mailing. Even though I only had a ninth-grade education, I wasn't unintelligent. In fact, many people didn't know that I had not finished high school, and I didn't tell them anything differently. I was a very good employee. I wanted to excel in my duties. Once again, I had a new lease on life, and I wanted to make the best of it. I was promoted as soon as my ninety-day probation had ended. It was a wonderful feeling working on my first *real* job and doing well at it.

Because I had a good-paying job, I was able to become more independent. My goal was to get my own place and create a new life for my boys and me. Andre was a little guy who seemed to have grown-up sense. Sometimes I believe I pushed him beyond normal limits. By the time he was ready for school, I had taught him so much. He knew the entire alphabet, how to count to one hundred, his address and telephone number, how to spell and write his own name, and how to tell time. He even learned how to tie his shoes with some initial difficulty.

Like my mother did with me, I didn't allow
Andre to say, "I can't." He was my little man of the
house. He protected and watched out for his little
brother's well-being. He realized that sometimes he
had to go without some things so that Tyree could
have what he needed. He truly was mother's little
helper, my little man who made my life a little easier.
Andre was very grown-up for such a little guy.

When Curtis got out of jail, his brother planned
a coming home party. Early that morning, his friend,
Edgar Moton, came over to the house to see if we
wanted to go with him to pick up Curtis. We all
packed into the car and rode to the L.A. County Jail.
To our surprise, Curtis had already been released and
was apparently on his way home by bus. I asked
Moton to take me home so I could be there when
Curtis came. After arriving home, Curtis called to say
that he was out of jail and had talked to Moton. He
advised me not to get in the car with Moton because it
was stolen. Little did he know that the kids and I had
already been in the car. I was amazed that Moton, a
friend of the family, would put the kids and me in that
kind of danger. I assured Curtis that I would not get in
the car with Moton again.

When Moton arrived, I told him that I wasn't ready to go, and that I would get there later. Curtis must have spent most of the morning seeing friends and family members. Later that afternoon, we got to see him. He spent the rest of the day with us. That night, we joined our friends and family members at the party. I noticed a change in Curtis. He wasn't really into the party. Maybe being in jail had made a difference. After a little bit of partying, Curtis was ready for us to go. His friends begged him to stay, but it seemed that being with the kids and me was more important to him than anything else. After leaving the party, we stopped at a store to buy some food, which included treats for Andre and Tyree. We then went to a motel room, where we stayed for the rest of the weekend. We spent a lot of time talking about how we were going to make a better life together.

First thing Monday morning, Curtis went out looking for a job. He was fortunate to find work right away. Once everything began to fall into place, we began to make wedding plans. We started by selecting the wedding party. I asked Bertie to be my maid-of-honor and Sharon, a good, new friend from work, to be my bridesmaid. Curtis' brother, Donald, was to be his best man, and his good friend, Mark, was his usher. Andre was the ring bearer and Taffylon, my old supervisor's daughter from NYC, was the flower girl. I made the two ladies' and the flower girl's dresses. My dress was custom-made. Because I tended to be somewhat flamboyant in the way I dressed, the design of my wedding dress was quite unique.

Curtis and I managed to save some money to buy furniture and other house necessities. We anticipated getting additional items that we needed for our home as wedding gifts. Our biggest challenge was finding a nice, affordable apartment in which to live. We were constantly disappointed after hours of looking, but we continued to look while making wedding plans.

On my wedding day, Curtis, Donald, and Mark were an hour late. As we all sat around waiting for them, Sharon helped take the edge off of everything with her humor. At one point, she said, "Don't worry, Verna. One monkey don't stop no show." Because she kept us laughing and joking the whole time, the hour passed fairly quickly. When the guys finally showed up, all of them, including Curtis, were drunk from partying all night. Despite that, they were able to get to the ceremony. The wedding was a funny experience.

Curtis' parents, who were always late, showed up with a movie camera just in time to film the tail end of the wedding. The reception was at their home. After we left the chapel, we headed there for the reception. Their home was beautifully decorated. The Crayons were very proud of their home and took pride in keeping it looking nice.

After the reception at the Crayons, one of our friends had an after party. Curtis and I stopped by briefly. When we got there, the Isley Brothers' hit song, "It's Your Thing," was playing. It was also playing when we left, although I don't recall if it played the whole time we were there. I was so happy; nothing else mattered. I had a family again.

My parents agreed to allow us to stay at their house until we found our own apartment. It took us about two weeks to find a place of our own. It was a nice, small apartment on 81st, between Figueroa and Hoover, in L.A. Curtis' grandmother let us use her car until we could afford to buy our own. I caught the bus to work, while Curtis used the car to get to his job. Getting to work by bus for him was more difficult. With the support of our family and our working together, the marriage got off to a really good start. We were able to purchase new furniture, open a bank account, and had the opportunity to use our wonderful wedding gifts. Things were working well. I was truly happy again.

As a parent, I was very strict. I constantly made sure that Andre and Tyree were well behaved. I wanted them to be near perfect. Even though they tried really hard, they couldn't always live up to my standards of perfection. When they did not, I had no problems punishing them. Tyree especially was always getting into some kind of trouble. Andre, on the other hand, would generally stay out of trouble. He loved his brother so much that he would never tattle on him.

We had lots of good times together. I took excellent care of my kids and performed all of my wifely duties. Curtis was a very loving and caring husband and dad, although at times, he got a little controlling. When that would occur, I was reminded of the abuse I had experienced with Theodore. While I did not think he could ever be as violent as Theodore, I had promised myself that I would never let anyone treat me like that ever again. When Curtis became controlling, I took a very defiant attitude, which led to some knock-down-drag-out arguments.

Because we were one of the few couples in our circle of friends who had a place of our own, people came over frequently. The constant company eventually became a problem for me because I found it difficult to get up in the morning after entertaining friends until the early morning hours. At times, after they left, Curtis and I argued until the wee hours of the morning, usually over little or nothing.

One evening, Curtis and I had an argument that turned so violent that I decided to take my children and leave. As I headed for the door, he grabbed my arm, causing me to lose my balance. As I fell, I struck my eye on the corner of a heavy, marble table. Needless to say, I was too hurt to leave that night.

The next morning, I awoke to find my left eye and the whole side of my face badly swollen. I couldn't go to work looking battered, but I had already been late and absent a few too many times. The telephone company had strict policies about too much absenteeism and tardiness. I tried to think of a good excuse for missing work so that I would not risk losing my job. I decided to tell my supervisor that my father had died. By the next day, flowers began arriving from my co-workers, and we got sympathy calls from people. As it turned out, I was dismissed anyway after they found out that I had lied. I felt bad that the lie got so out of hand. I also felt badly about using my father as an excuse.

In an instant, we turned into a one-income household and things started to get a little tough. Being at home did allow me to spend more time with the children. But, I needed a job because we needed the additional money. I convinced myself that it wasn't the end of the world and that we could get through this rough spot. Then, I found out that I was pregnant again.

The stress from arguing and fighting with Curtis took its toll on me. As a result, I delivered another premature baby, this time in my sixth month. We named him Curtis Alexander II. Because his lungs were not fully developed, he was unable to breathe properly. Because of these and other complications, he died the day after he was born. While this marked another sad day in my life, I was thankful that he didn't have to go through the agony of being spastic, as the doctor said would have happened, had he survived. I felt that God had taken away my son for a reason.

We barely had enough income to pay our bills and purchase our necessities because I still wasn't working. Shortly after the baby died, we were forced to move to a less expensive place on Parmelee Street, near Central Avenue and Imperial Highway. I hoped that the move would be temporary because it was not an area that was fit for raising two young children. We had no other choice; we had to make do until we could do better. Not long after the move, I began pounding the pavement in search of another job. Once again, God was looking out for me. During my job search, I answered a want ad for a position in the credit department at Sears and Roebuck. I filled out the necessary paperwork, took a test, and was hired immediately.

Andre, five and his brother, Tyree, two.

CHAPTER 10

My Jobs

aphne, the girlfriend of one of Curtis' friends, agreed to baby-sit Andre and Tyree. Her house was convenient to my new job. Each morning, Curtis dropped the kids and me off at Daphne's house on his way to work. I would have time for a quick nap, after which I would freshen up and leave to catch the bus to my new job.

My job as a credit correspondent was a good experience. I worked with a group of very interesting co-workers, and I also met an array of interesting customers. At the end of each day, I left with the feeling that I could do any job in the company. I soaked up all the knowledge that I could and enjoyed my work very much. But, I only kept this job for approximately six months.

During the first few months that Daphne began keeping the boys, I noticed that Andre was extremely hungry when we got home, and that Tyree had severe diaper rash. This seemed odd because I always left plenty of food, snacks, and diapers with Daphne. I concluded that she obviously was not doing a good job of baby-sitting my children. I needed a baby-sitter in order to continue working. Finding out that the person that we had chosen was not doing a good job presented a real problem.

One day, I looked in Daphne's cabinets to find all of the food that I had been bringing piled high. I confronted her about what I had found. She agreed to do better. But my mind was already made up. At that point, I immediately began to search for another baby-sitter.

I soon learned that all of the Sears credit files were being sent to the new office location in Torrance. I also found out that computers would perform my job. While Sears offered everyone in my department the opportunity to transfer to the new location, it was simply too far for me to travel by bus. Sears offered several people who could not transfer different positions at the present location, but I wasn't one of them because I had not been working there long enough. The remainder of us were laid off, which, considering my childcare issues, I really didn't mind. For a little while at least, I would have the opportunity to stay home with Andre and Tyree. I vowed that before I would seek employment again, my first priority would be to find a reliable baby-sitter.

While I enjoyed staying at home, my not working meant that we had money problems once again. What little savings we did have quickly whittled away. We were forced to uproot once again. I didn't mind leaving the apartment, but I was certain that if we couldn't afford where we were, we sure couldn't afford anything better. We ended up in a one-bedroom apartment on 82nd Street, between Figueroa and Hoover. I hoped that this move would be temporary and that things would turn around for us soon.

Our first day on 82nd Street, I noticed three little girls at an apartment across the street who looked familiar. I learned that they were my cousin Lois' daughters. I was pleasantly surprised to find that I had relatives living directly across the street. And, ironically, my friend Bobbie moved next door to Lois in a duplex that she shared with another friend, Shirley. My sister-in-law Elaine also moved down the street with her family. Knowing so many people in the community was very comforting.

I soon became the neighborhood baby-sitter. I also took care of my brother-in-law's children, Pookie and Yvette, for nine months while their mother was in jail. Sometimes, I would baby-sit Curtis' youngest brother, Daryl, who was Andre's age. Our apartment seemed to be a haven for kids. At times, there would be so many kids in the house that I had to be sure to count them all when I called them in to eat.

In addition to caring for children, sewing also became a source of income for me, just as it had been for my mother and grandmother. My new sewing customers helped to supplement my unemployment benefits.

When the time finally came for Andre to start school, both he and I were excited. I made plans to sew all of his clothes. He was going to be the best-dressed boy in the whole school. I started sewing over the summer so that by the time school started, all of his clothes would be ready to wear. In those days, vests and pants suits were the "in thing." In addition to sewing for Andre, I also sewed dresses for my niece, Yvette. I made sure that they all dressed nicely for school. Pookie wore Andre's hand-me-downs, who then passed them down to Tyree.

I would get the cloth from a small fabric store on Vermont Avenue. Then I would select from remnant pieces of fabric in a wide array of colors. I spent hours making different styles of clothing. I made so many clothes that Andre was able to wear a different pants suit to school everyday. I always received compliments from the kids' teacher and even other parents about how well-dressed Andre was. The compliments from other people made us both very proud. The teachers also complimented us on how well-disciplined he was.

Andre was an all-around excellent student. My being home with him so much in the beginning gave him a jump start academically. It also helped Andre realize how much I really loved him, which gave him confidence to go out to face this new world of strange people at school. He always received good grades, quickly earning the respect of his teachers.

Once he got settled in school, I was still faced with the issue of our living conditions. We didn't live there too long, but long enough to see lots of dramas and have sad memories. For instance, a pair of women who were drug addicts lived there. They often stumbled down the street. And in one of the apartments across the street from us, the owner had converted a small recreation room into a neighborhood nightclub, which drew its share of characters. We also had a host of women, whom I called the *county (welfare) women*, staying in nearby housing. These women had men who hung around them only at or near the first and fifteenth of each month. In addition to these things, lots of children gathered outside to play. Some of them were bad, and some of their parents were even worse.

One day, I watched two kids who were approximately three years old get into a little scuffle. The mothers' solution to the problem was to meet outside, armed with knives, and fight it out themselves. While they fought, the two kids had made up and gone back to playing. Afterwards, the mothers forbade the kids from playing together ever again. As I witnessed this encounter from my window, I recalled thinking what a wonderful world this would be if adults could resolve their differences the way kids do. Andre and Tyree played with the children that I baby-sat. So, I didn't have to worry about getting into an altercation with neighborhood moms.

One morning, I got the sad news that my grand-mother on my mom's side had passed away. I cried so much that day whenever I thought about my grand-mother being gone. She was 83 years old, but I guess I expected her to live forever. The day of her funeral was one of the saddest days of my life. I still miss her so much.

The night after the funeral, the shaking of my bed woke me up. Then I felt what seemed like a cold hand on my back, attempting to keep me from rising. When I got up, I looked to see if Andre or Tyree had gotten into bed with me, but I found them fast asleep. As I gazed out of the bedroom door, I saw an image in pink go past. I remembered that my grandmother was wearing pink as she lay in the casket. A creepy feeling suddenly came over me. I knew I couldn't leave the house because the kids were asleep. I didn't know where I would go anyway. I couldn't go back to sleep, so I went outside to sit on the porch until Curtis returned home from his mother's house.

For several months after that, I would occasion-ally feel the bed moving. I simply got used to it, and I never mentioned it to Curtis. I wondered if he ever felt the bed moving, too. But since he never mentioned anything about it, I just kept it to myself. I don't recall being afraid. I merely concluded that my grandmother was just checking on me, as she would often do when she lived at my parents' house.

When I was younger, she would come into my bedroom and warmly and softly touch my back. This made me feel safe, secure, and loved. Sometimes when she came in, I wouldn't move, even though I knew she was there. I would just smile to myself, enjoying the fact she was there for me.

At this point in my life, I had become a homebody, wife, and mother. Besides my children and sewing, the only other interest that I had was music. I had a phenomenal record collection. Music was always playing in the house. I cleaned house to music. I had my best thoughts while listening to music. And, I lived by certain words from certain songs. When people dropped by, they sometimes thought that there was a party going on. But it was just the boys, my music, and me. After Andre learned how to play the records, I would occasionally let him deejay for me and for our company. Even then, he was really good. Andre learned to recognize record labels even before he could read by looking at the color of the label or other distinguishing features.

One day as I was getting ready to go to the fabric store, Bobbie and Shirley stopped by to advise me that there was a new retail store called National Dollar opening on Vermont, near Manchester. They were both planning to apply for jobs there and wanted me to join them. I told them that I would walk with them since I was going that way. Once we got to the new store, they convinced me to stop there with them to complete an application, after which I went to the fabric store. No sooner than I got home, I received a call from the store manager, offering me an interview. I was so excited that I ran across the street to tell Bobbie and Shirley that I had a call about the position and to see if they got a call as well. They had not. At that very moment, I remembered some advice that my mother had given me—"Never take a friend with you when you're applying for a job; the friend may get the job, and you may not." I went in for an interview and was immediately hired. Shirley and Bobbie were a little upset because they were the ones really looking for a job. They got over it eventually and were very happy for me. Even though neither of them received a call, Shirley continued to try to get a job there and was eventually hired. Bobbie searched for jobs at other places.

My new employment was not totally good news to some of my other friends because it meant that they would have to find someone else to watch their children. It was really bittersweet for me because I truly loved watching children. However, I couldn't afford to pass up more money. My new job was within walking distance from home, and my hours were the opposite of Curtis', so we didn't even need a baby-sitter to watch the boys.

Now that we had a little more income coming into the household, we thought it was time to look for a bigger place in a better environment. We were able to find a place nearby on 83rd Street, between Hoover and Vermont. It was a nice, roomy, three-bedroom back house (a house in back of a small house). Later, I was concerned that we had settled on a place too soon. Shirley moved in the apartment building next door to our house. We both thought that this was a better neighborhood, but that proved not to be true. During the first three months, Shirley's house got burglarized three times. We were fortunate not to get hit because either Curtis or I were always home. But we were concerned because the bigger kids that lived in the front house always picked fights with Andre and Tyree. And, there was a group of undesirable people that were constantly hanging around. Eventually, Shirley and I both bought guns for our protection.

I continued to walk to and from work, but that soon became a problem because of the roving gangs of youth. One night when I had almost reached home, a car drove up beside me, and two guys demanded that I throw them my purse. Without hesitation, I pulled out my gun and aimed it at them. They sped away. I waited until they were out of sight before running home so they wouldn't see where I lived. I knew then that I would have to move, so I immediately began making plans. The final straw came when I returned home one evening to find that my house had been burglarized while Curtis and the boys had gone shopping. Besides that, I was totally fed up with living in other people's places. I wanted us to find a home of our own. I began exploring the possibility of buying a house where my kids could have their own yard, and we could have peace of mind.

We didn't have any money saved, but we were still determined to become homeowners. So I started saving the money that I made from sewing, and both Curtis and I began putting away a little money at a time from our jobs. Before long, we found a house that we wanted to buy. To my surprise, we qualified for a mortgage on the first try, and, before we knew it, we were being handed the keys to our new home. We had a great feeling of accomplishment. We had worked hard as a family to realize a common goal. At twenty-three years old, my husband and I had become homeowners. At a young age, I had accomplished what took my parents many years to do. I felt that I could do anything. I had come a long way from those high school days filled with bad decisions. We were adults, who had made grown-up decisions. I felt good about the whole thing.

Our new house was located on Imperial Highway, a few blocks from Central Avenue. Andre, who was seven years old, transferred to the school in that area. Our old faithful baby-sitter, who lived across the street from my parents' house, once again agreed to watch the boys. I taught Andre how to catch the bus to and from school and to the baby-sitter across the street from my mother's house. Shortly after the move, I was transferred to my job's El Segundo and Avalon location, which was closer to our home.

One day, the baby-sitter called me at work to say that Andre hadn't made it in from school. I left work frantic, thinking the worst. I got a ride to my parents' house, and we went out searching for Andre. After a few hours of looking everywhere that we thought he might be, we stopped back by the baby-sitter's house to find that Andre was there. He told us that a man had taken him away from the bus stop and gave us a description of the man. We went looking for the stranger, but upon further questioning, Andre finally admitted he had gone off with a friend to play at a nearby park. This was so unlike him. He always followed instructions very well and had never done anything except what was expected of him. But like any child, I had to realize that he could sometimes do wrong. I gave him a sermon about how bad things can happen to kids who wander off. He got the same lecture from my parents and the baby-sitter, too. He saw how upset we were and promised to never do that again.

Andre finished the year at school with no more problems. The following school year, we transferred him to Mark Twain Elementary School, which was within walking distance from the baby-sitter's house.

I had a lot more peace of mind knowing that he could walk to and from school with the kids in my parents' neighborhood. Andre continued to get good grades throughout his years in elementary school. We established a new transportation plan whereby I would catch the bus with Andre and Tyree in the mornings to the baby-sitter's house and walk one block to the shopping center where my job was located. When my mom got home in the evening, she would go across the street, get Andre and Tyree, and take them to her house. By the time I got off work, my mom had already let them play, had fed them dinner, and had made sure that Andre had done his homework. When I arrived, we would all catch the bus from my mom's house home.

Andre's First Grade picture.

CHAPTER 11

Divorce & Reconciliation

After several years of stable employment, Curtis lost his job. I didn't know the reason, and he didn't want to talk about it. Curtis' unemployment led once again to marital discord. We argued and fought often. We had come so close to making this thing work and now this . . . Curtis started spending a lot of time away from home, hanging out with friends, drinking, and doing drugs. After one too many arguments, I decided to ask for a divorce.

Curtis was not happy at all about my decision. During one of our arguments, he actually threatened to take his own life by locking himself in the garage with the car running. It was a horrible night. I called my mom, who came over to talk him out of doing something so crazy and to convince him to stop scaring us with those threats. The kids and I packed up and went to stay with my parents. While I was there, I consulted with an attorney about filing for a divorce. I was truly fed up, and this time, I wanted out. Curtis was a good-hearted man who was always there for the kids and me. I could deal with his drinking because I drank occasionally. But, I couldn't handle his drug use. I had always heard about how difficult it is to get a person off drugs after they are hooked. I didn't want to drag my kids or myself through that for Curtis or any other man. While Curtis had not become a habitual user, I felt he was well on his way to becoming one. Most of his friends drank and used drugs. Whenever he was with them, he would come home high.

He promised to stop using drugs and limit his visits with friends if the kids and I returned home. I decided to give him another chance. So we moved back. But the arguments and fights became so violent that I asked him to leave. If he cared so little about his own life to want to end it, how could I trust him with my children's lives or mine?

Under the divorce decree, I was awarded custody of the kids and the house. I attempted to go on with my life. Curtis continued to harass me with threats of violence so much so that I finally took out a restraining order against him. I couldn't handle paying for a house where I couldn't live comfortably. And while I hated to, I had to walk away. However, since I had come from strong stock, I was convinced that I would be bent, but not broken. My grandparents had made it. My parents made it. And, I was going to make it, too!

I immediately began to look for an apartment for the boys and me. Bobbie told me about a new apartment complex that was in the final stages of construction. She and I both applied for one of the units. While waiting for the apartment to be completed, I was able to save money and develop a new survival plan for my family. The apartment complex, which was gated and guarded, was located in the city of Compton, at the corner of Laurel Street and Wilmington Avenue. When it was first built, it was a safe environment for the kids and me. Our apartment had three bedrooms, so both boys could have their own room. Andre and Tyree still chose to share a bedroom because they wanted to be close to one another. We used the other bedroom as a den to entertain company.

I always kept a clean house, and I taught Andre and Tyree to do likewise. Even as little boys, I gave them chores. Andre felt he was the man of the house at a very young age. Although he was too young to take on all the responsibilities of a man, he did his best to look out for us. If someone entered our house that he didn't feel comfortable with, he would remain close by me until the person was gone. I laid down very strict rules for my sons regarding manners, appearance, and their education. I expected nothing less than the best from them in whatever they did.

While I had many male friends, I was not intimate with any of them at this point. I wanted to be a good mother. My friends came by quite frequently, but only when they had something to give us. I guess they realized that I truly was a struggling mother; one determined to get ahead, even if it meant struggling by myself. My number one goal in life was *to succeed*.

One of my friends would come over almost every Friday to take me to the record store. He knew I loved music. Because of his generosity, I had the largest record collection of all my friends. My refrigerator stayed full of juices, sodas, and milk. Friends would bring beer and wine for themselves and to share with me.

Bobbie moved into the same apartment complex soon after we did. Her apartment was in the same section as ours. She was the single parent of a daughter named Valissa. We looked out for one another. She was at my place all the time. After a while, I grew tired of having company every night because I missed spending time alone with Andre and Tyree. Eventually, I sometimes resorted to not answering the doorbell when friends came by. I would look through the peephole first. If it wasn't my mom or dad, I did not answer the door.

One evening after work, I walked to my parents' house. I was thinking about asking my mom to watch the boys for me because my friends asked me to go to a party. Because I had not entertained company in a while, I really wanted to accept the offer. Mom agreed to watch the boys and even offered to drive me home instead of me taking the bus.

My dad and the boys rode with us so that they could accompany my mom back home. I sat in the front seat with mom while dad sat in the backseat with Andre and Tyree. As we approached the corner of Wilmington and Laurel Street, mom inched up to the middle of the intersection to make a left turn onto Laurel Street. When the light turned red for the oncoming traffic, she proceeded to make her turn. At that moment, I saw a car speeding toward us like a bat out of hell. I started yelling, "Momma! Momma! Momma!" as I braced myself for the impact. The car crashed into us with such force that we spun around and landed on the curb on the opposite side of the street. My first instinct was check to see if everyone was okay. Mom appeared to be a little shaken and disoriented, but was unharmed. Dad was okay, too. I could hear Tyree frantically screaming the whole time, but I couldn't tell whether he was hurt or just scared.

As I was making sure that he wasn't hurt, I looked to make sure Andre was alright. When I scanned the car, I didn't see him. I jumped out of the car, frantically yelling out to him. A police officer arrived on the scene, opened the back door of the car, and pulled him out from under the seat. I was hysterical when I saw that my child had blood on his face and wasn't moving.

Andre had gone to sleep with his head against the window. The impact of the crash threw him to the other side of the car. The broken glass from the window cut several gashes in his face. Tyree suffered a minor cut to the back of his head. The officer didn't wait for an ambulance. Instead, he put me, Andre, and Tyree in the patrol car and rushed us to the hospital. The nearest hospital for trauma victims was Dominguez Valley Hospital. My mom and dad remained at the scene to exchange information with the driver of the other vehicle and the police.

I called Bobbie, who picked up my parents to bring them to the hospital. Andre was in terrible pain. As his mother, I felt every bit of it. He acted very mature, however, as a doctor stitched up the gashes on his face. I was happy he was not more seriously injured, but I prayed that the cuts would not leave permanent scars. Thank God, we were all able to go home that night.

I got the boys settled in bed for the night, knowing they probably would not sleep well. Then I sat around awhile, talking with Bobbie and my parents back at their house. I was reminded that night what a wonderful friend Bobbie was. She was always there for me, just as I was for her. I had forgotten all about the party. Instead, I spent the night watching Andre and Tyree.

It had been a year since I had seen Curtis. I called him the next day to let him know what had happened. He wanted to make sure the boys were okay. While I didn't need any more drama in my life, I thought that it was only right that I allow him to see them under the circumstances. I recalled also that the restraining order was still in effect. I weighed the situation and finally decided that a father should be allowed the privilege of seeing his kids at a time like this.

After that day, Curtis began visiting regularly. The boys were always so happy to see their daddy that I didn't complain about the fact that he was violating the restraining order. After Andre began to complain about pain in his chest and I noticed that he had begun to favor one side after the accident, Curtis and I decided to take him to a doctor. Curtis' family's doctor, Dr. Anderson, examined him. An x-ray diagnosed a broken collarbone. The x-rays that were taken the night of the accident were said to have been clear. Later, I received a letter which stated that after a more thorough check, they found abnormalities. Under Dr. Anderson's watch, however, Andre got the best possible care for his injury.

He handled the pain for his injury so well. I wondered if that was because I had taught him the importance of enduring pain when he would complain about simple aches and pains from small cuts and bruises. Or, maybe it was Andre's nature to remain cool and calm under pressure. That personality trait has been his trademark to this day.

As Curtis' visits continued, he began hinting about us getting back together. I was very reluctant to do so because I had really gotten used to the peace of mind of not constantly fussing and fighting. There was no way that I wanted to put the boys and me through that again. I must admit that we could have used Curtis' financial help. In those days, it was difficult to collect child support, and I didn't even try. When people divorced, they went on their merry way. At times, we were so strapped for cash that I would search between the cushions and empty out my purses, searching for change to buy dinner.

Curtis eventually convinced me to take him back. He had to do a lot of talking, begging, pleading, and promising to do the right thing before I agreed to it. I finally consented to try it again. I was scared to death, not for my safety, but that we would fail again. While I was on my own, I managed to buy new furniture for the boys' room and the living room. I had also placed a dining room set and bar in layaway. As his first gesture of goodwill, Curtis got the dining room set and bar out of layaway.

Our apartment looked like a picture out of an interior-decorating magazine. The living room and kitchen were nicely decorated with white furniture trimmed in black with red accents. The master bedroom had a round, blue velvet headboard and footstool against a round waterbed. People often wondered how I managed to keep everything so neat with small children. They just didn't know that Andre and Tyree were exactly like their mother. They, too, had grown to like nice things. I felt that having children should not deny a person the privilege of having nice things. After all, our having nice things at home taught the boys to respect other people's nice things.

Curtis and I got along wonderfully for a while, except for the fact that he constantly asked me to consider re-marrying him, a subject that I kept evading. Marriage always seemed to be where my problems started. As a woman, I think I expected too much from marriage. And, as a result, I made some bad decisions. I didn't want to go through that again. So we continued to live together.

This picture taken on the steps of Providence Missionary Baptist Church. My Mom and Dad were both Ushers. They are both on the right end.

CHAPTER 12

My Accident
& My Education

We spent a lot of time doing things as a family. We went on camping trips to Lake Isabella and Salton Sea, along with Curtis' parents. His parents took care of all the details for the trip, such as reserving trailers, choosing the date, and reserving the campsites. The trailer company was responsible for placing trailers at the site.

When we first began going on the trips, our group consisted of my family, Curtis' parents, his younger brother Darryl, his sister Elaine, her family, his brother Donald, and his family. As time went on, the trips became popular and other friends and family members joined us for the fun.

Curtis' dad rode a motorcycle and was a member of a club called *The L.A. Rattlers*. Once a year, many of the motorcycle clubs in the U.S. held a large gathering at what was called the Salton Sea Run. Each year we looked forward to going down to Salton Sea for the event. There were hundreds of fine bikes and lots of beautiful people. It was exciting to see all the variety of motorcycle clubs with their members wearing sharp jean vests and leather jackets having the clubs' names on the back as everyone sat proudly on their bikes, rolling down the highway two by two. It seemed as if the long parade of bikes owned the road. I loved hearing the sound of the cycles as they entered the campsite. To me, it sounded like a continuous roar of thunder, coupled with the beat of a bass drum. What club members called the "heavy throttle" shook the earth beneath my feet like a small earthquake. The constant roar was in the air all weekend. The air was also filled with loud conversations and heavy laughter.

I remember one Salton Sea trip in particular in the summer of 1975. This trip was certain to be lots of fun because so many of our friends and family members were going. We all loaded up in cars, vans, a camper, and a pickup truck that carried our bikes and the cases of beer, which Curtis' dad always provided. When we arrived, we began our usual routine of unpacking the cars, organizing things in our trailers, and getting the kids bedded down. The adults stayed up to enjoy the rest of the night, laughing, talking, and drinking until one by one, everyone eventually went to bed.

The next morning, Curtis' brother, Donald, discovered that he had lost his keys, possibly at the gas station where we had stopped on the way. He and his wife Hithia decided to ride one of the motorcycles back to the gas station to search for the keys. Curtis followed them on another motorcycle. He asked me to go with him. I refused at first because I had a lots to do to prepare the campsite. After much prodding, I finally agreed.

The ride was wonderful. I enjoyed the morning air blowing through my hair and the wind in my face. *This is the life*, I thought to myself. I believe we were going about ninety miles an hour when suddenly, Donald saw a bunch of bikers at a roadside stop and decided he wanted to turn off the highway to join them. This was a two-lane highway. Instead of signaling that he was going to turn, Donald sped ahead of us and turned directly in front of us. We had two choices. We could either make the sudden turn with him or go around into the oncoming lane, smack into a diesel truck. As Donald completed the turn, he stopped to see if we were still with him. We made the turn right behind him. Because he stopped, we were forced to plow right into him as we came out of the turn. I immediately flew off the bike and into the air. I don't remember much of what happened beyond that point, but I do recall that after I slid, rolled, and flipped, I ended up at the bottom of a ditch. I may have lost consciousness for a few seconds. But then I slowly regained my hearing, sight, and feelings. I could hear people asking if I was alright, in addition to mumbles and other sounds. When my vision began to clear up, I could see people standing around me. By the looks on their faces, it seemed that I was hurt pretty badly. After the feeling returned to my body, I felt an excruciating pain, which was my signal for just how badly hurt I really was.

Hithia, Donald, and Curtis were also hurt, although not as badly as I was. After the paramedics arrived, we were taken through the winding mountain roads to the nearest hospital in a small town called Indio, California. The trip seemed to take forever, probably because I was in so much pain. When we arrived, I was rushed directly into emergency to begin treatment of my injuries. I suffered a laceration to the forehead and asphalt burns to my left thigh and arm. Anyone who has ever had an asphalt burn knows it can feel more painful than a fire burn. I had gravel embedded in my thigh and arms, which had to be removed piece by piece. Lord only knows what a truly painful experience that was to endure. The denim from my jeans, which was also embedded in my skin, had to be scrubbed out. More pain. To me, getting burned is just as bad as being in labor, as far as the level of pain goes.

After several hospital attendants, doctors, and nurses finished poking, picking, and probing my body, I was bandaged to the point that I resembled a mummy. Then I was forced to spend the duration of the weekend in the hospital.

When I was discharged, we returned to Curtis' parents' home. Bobbie had told my folks that I had been hurt in the motorcycle accident. They came by to see me and were distraught to find me in that condition. My mother recommended that I go to her doctor until I was completely healed and able to return to work.

After two years at National Dollar, I was growing tired of working at what seemed to be a dead-end job. So, I decided to look for a position elsewhere. I wanted to leave before I got too comfortable. I began responding to want ads in the classified section of several local newspapers. I also registered at the State Employment Office and made cold calls to some companies that featured help wanted signs in windows or on buildings. I filled out application after application, took test after test, and went on many interviews. When I wasn't successful, I concluded that something was preventing me from getting a better job. Obtaining a job had always been a piece of cake for me in the past. It used to be that I would complete the application, go to the interview, and before I knew it, I was offered the job.

After many disappointments, I finally got a job at K-Mart Department Store, on Western Avenue and Imperial Highway. I found myself back in the same old rut, performing the same tasks that I had at National Dollar. I examined the reasons for the rejections and why it had not been as easy to get good positions as previously before I ended up at National Dollar Store. I wondered what was holding me back. Before, all I needed was some high school education with a few skills to land a good job. Now they were looking for applicants with high school diplomas or technical training, as well as skills. So I decided that the best thing for me to do was to go back to school to get some additional training.

When I spoke to Curtis about the idea, he was totally against it. I wondered why and discovered after a few discussions that he was very insecure. He feared that I would get an education, a real good job, and would not need him anymore. I thought it was ridiculous for him to think that way. After all, whatever I did for the betterment of my financial status would be shared with him as well.

Despite his objections, I was determined to increase my level of education. And so, I enrolled in Webster Career College's legal secretary program. The college would allow me to take classes to prepare for the GED and had grant programs to assist in paying my tuition and transportation. I had to ride three buses to and from school. I didn't mind that inconvenience because I was so excited about this new challenge in my life. I knew that higher education was the key to my future success.

I enrolled Tyree in the same school that Andre attended. Curtis agreed to see to it that the boys got to and from school everyday. Because he wasn't happy about my decision, in some ways he made things difficult for me on a daily basis. Overall, though, going to school went smoothly.

While I was at Webster, I met lots of new and interesting people. The teachers took an interest in the students and encouraged them in every way possible. I took advantage of their support. I focused on my studies and worked hard to get the best grades possible. Believe me, it wasn't easy. With two young boys and a meager income, we barely survived.

Webster Career College had been a modeling school before becoming a career college. Some of the instructors from the modeling school continued to teach business etiquette and other courses. These instructors also ran an after-school modeling program, which I received a scholarship to be a part of, along with a few other students who had strong grade point averages.

Because I was tall and slender, I had been approached many times by modeling agents prior to me enrolling in the program at Webster. But Curtis discouraged me from pursuing a modeling career. In fact, the mere thought of me interacting with a male on a one-on-one basis sent him into a rage. To be honest, I was easily discouraged because I lacked self-confidence. But since the school had offered me this opportunity, I wasn't going to let it pass me by this time. I was quite eager to learn. I had gotten into a "groove" in my life and was soaking up all the education I could.

I wished that Curtis were just slightly excited and even more than just a little supportive of my efforts. But I knew that the only thing that would make him happy was for me to quit. He would have probably planned a party the same night if I had done that. I jumped right into modeling. To my surprise, the walks, the turns, and everything else came very easily for me. In fact, my instructors called me a natural. I kept going to the modeling classes until I finished the legal secretary course. I finished the nine-month course in seven months, with a 4.0 grade point average. On my graduation day, my parents, my two boys, and several of my friends sat proudly in the audience. I can still remember the keynote speech, even though I don't remember the name of the speaker.

The speaker told a story about a guy whom he knew from high school that had been popular because of his ability to dance well and to charm the ladies by dancing with a scarf. While dancing, he would wrap the scarf around his partner, fling it in the air, turning, then catching it and doing other little gestures. He remained popular throughout high school as a result of his ability to be entertaining. Many years later, the speaker returned home to visit his family and ran into his classmate, who was wearing the same clothes and doing the same outdated dance with what looked like the same scarf. The moral of the story was that the guy was so concerned about clowning his way into popularity, he forgot that education was more important. The same people whom he danced with and performed for had left him behind. And while this guy still received laughs and a little bit of money for what he did, his classmates received a salary. I remembered thinking, *What a wonderful and meaningful speech.* I thought back to the days when I was the class clown and was glad those days were over. The speech gave me even more encouragement to make something of my life.

When it came time for me to get my diploma, I looked at Andre and Tyree, who sat bright-eyed with anticipation at hearing their mommy's name called as I walked across the stage. When I heard my name and the applause that followed, I felt so good to be receiving that diploma, as well as an honor award. Although I really hadn't expected to see him, I still was disappointed when Curtis didn't show up on my big day. I even looked around the room, hoping that he might have come late.

I thought about how opposed he was to my striving so hard to achieve this goal and how hard he tried to tear me down. In the end, not only did I not allow Curtis' hang-ups to discourage me from making this great accomplishment, I could boast that I was one of the best.

I am deeply appreciative for the second chance that I received at Webster College. I left there with a new walk and a new way of communicating. I had developed a new attitude and the confidence that I needed to accomplish even more in my life.

Shameka Denee Crayon, 6 months old.

CHAPTER 13

The Birth of Shameka
& More Problems

fter we had lived in the apartment on Laurel Street for nearly five years, Andre began attending Vanguard Junior High School, the same school that I had attended. Then his grades started to drop in some of his subjects. As a result, I received calls and notes from his teachers about his lack of interest in some of his subjects and his truancy. A number of times, our neighbors reported seeing Andre sitting on my parents' front porch during school hours. He was losing interest in school and was failing to attend. I was very upset, but I knew there must be a reason for this. Instead of

hollering at him, I remained calm so that I could determine the cause.

Andre was very quiet and always kept any problems he had to himself. I had to pay close attention to him to know if he wasn't feeling well or to know if something was bothering him, because he just wouldn't say. I often noticed that if he liked a subject, he would do well in it, and if he didn't like the subject, he would put forth very little effort. Although that was probably typical for students his age, it was unacceptable to me. I began calmly counseling him about the importance of getting good grades in all subjects and about how missing school could be a major problem. He responded well to my approach and began trying to bring his grades up in all his classes. He stopped skipping school, but the problems continued.

Andre had typically done well in math. But one day, I got a letter from the principal's office, stating that the teacher wanted to meet with me about Andre. When I got there, I just knew that he was in some kind of trouble. As he and I sat in the office waiting for the conference to begin, one of his teachers, Mr. Wright (my former teacher at Mark Twain), rushed into the office and noticed Andre and me sitting there. He said, "Silverson, how are you?" I responded that I was fine. He then looked at Andre and said, "Is he yours?" to which I replied, "Yes." Then, "Now I see why this kid is so sharp." I was relieved to know that I wasn't being summoned to resolve a problem. Instead, Mr. Wright had called me to say that Andre was too advanced for his current math class, and that he wanted to put him in a special class to learn a higher level of math.

I was relieved to know that Andre's difficulty in school was only due to a lack of interest. He was simply bored and needed more challenge. I consented to the change immediately and was so grateful to Mr. Wright.

After the problems with Andre's education were resolved, I began to concentrate on the many problems that were occurring in my personal life. First, we had begun to have problems at the apartment complex where we lived. After the apartment complex took on new management, our nice, safe, and quiet surroundings changed drastically. In fact, one night, we returned home to find that our apartment had been burglarized. Andre's bike and my record collection were among the items stolen. Losing those particular items hurt more than anything else. Andre had only ridden his bike once; it was brand-new. And, many of the records in my collection were irreplaceable.

Also, my boys also began to have problems with some of the new kids in the apartment complex. My sons meant everything to me; I was not going to reside in an atmosphere that was uncomfortable for them. I began considering the idea of moving once again. Not only did I want to buy a house in a nice neighborhood, but also I wanted to find a job with medical benefits.

Searching for the house was first on our list. It took approximately three months to locate the house I wanted. It was a two-bedroom house with an enormous den and a great big backyard for the kids. It was located on Mayo Street, in Compton. I had earned enough money for a down payment and got the house financed.

It was located in a very nice neighborhood. The other homes were well-kept, and we were surrounded by a wonderful group of neighbors. Andre began attending Roosevelt Junior High School, which was located a few blocks from our house. Tyree continued going to Mark Twain School.

After we found the house, I started looking for a better job. I began my job search like a soldier, armed with my diploma, letters of recommendation from the teachers at Webster, and a positive attitude. The search for a job was very short. Because I needed the income, I had to settle for one of the first positions that was offered to me. I remembered what my mom used to say, "A bird in the hand is worth two in the bush." I could do better later.

I was hired at Austin Bradlee Company as a general clerk. This company supplied personalized gifts for other companies' employees on their birthdays. We had lots of employees in our files from many companies. We would pull the employees names in their birthday months, note the gifts that had been selected for them, engrave their names on the gifts, and make sure they received the gifts on their birthdays.

The company was very small. Only eight employees, including the president, three clerks, an engraver, two shipping clerks, and two salespersons worked there. Like a family, we worked and blended well together. While I enjoyed working there, deep in my heart, I knew that I had not gone to school to end up with a job paying me twenty-five cents more than I had made working for K-Mart.

During my second month on the job, I discovered I was pregnant with my fifth and, what I hoped would be, my last child. I was reluctant to tell my boss that I was expecting since I had only been there for a short while. And, I wasn't sure what the company policy was as it related to pregnant employees. When I finally got up enough nerve to tell him, I was relieved to find that he was very understanding. In fact, he congratulated me. I was glad that work wasn't a problem, but I was still concerned about the hardship that having another child would present to my home life. I would eventually have to take maternity leave, which would ultimately present financial problems. But my mom always said, "The Lord never put a mouth here that He couldn't feed." With that in mind, I continued to work and decided that I would cross that bridge when the time came.

Curtis and I were still party people, although we had calmed down from the way it used to be. It was not uncommon for friends and relatives to drop by anytime, unannounced. A few people would come over and before you knew it, we had a house full. The guys would all group together in one room, laughing and discussing the world's problems, while the ladies would gather in another room, usually the kitchen, to have their own discussions. Both groups would eventually "dollar up" enough money to buy refreshments for snacks and drinks. Someone would go pick up what we needed. The kids would have fun playing in the den.

Andre would do what he enjoyed—which was spinning the records. Our friends would sometimes give him a dollar or two for his efforts.

People had begun to form van clubs all over the place. Our group of friends decided we needed to do the same. With the help of my parents who helped us cash in on an old life insurance policy, Curtis and I purchased our first van. Pretty soon, all the guys in our little circle had purchased vans. We were able to form a club of our own. We held several meetings to discuss the logistics of creating the club. After a short debate, we decided on the name "All For One Van Club." We chose that name because the members of our club were all family and friends—thus, one family.

Whereas before we used to go camping, we now began traveling from one place to another on what were called *van runs*. The van runs were competitive and lots of fun. We would compete against other van clubs in relay races. There were contests for the kids, for the ladies, and for the men. Some of the contests were co-ed. Winners received trophies. Our club took home many trophies.

At the van runs, each club would form a circle that resembled the old wagon train camps. All the clubs were welcome to visit one another's circles. The best part of these outings was that everyone, regardless of race, age, or gender, partied together the entire weekend. There were no incidents. There was nothing but pure unadulterated fun.

On the weekends that we were not on van runs, we spent time raising money for the next one by having house parties. Our family and another family, the Morgans, hosted most of the house parties because our homes had the most space. We sponsored other fund-raising events as well. Some of the more successful ones were the Hot Goblin Jam (a Halloween party) and our San Diego Jazz Festival Run, which took place in the spring every year at Jack Murphy Stadium, in San Diego. Our van club would book rooms at hotels for the entire weekend. These van club events were truly the highlight of my life.

We scheduled a party on November 14, 1976, at our house. At that time, I was nine months pregnant. On Sunday afternoon, the week before the house party, Curtis and I were entertaining a member of the van club and his wife when I felt a little pain. I went quickly to the bathroom where I stayed a while. As soon as I returned, I felt another pain and left the room again. No one questioned my frequent trips to the bathroom, maybe because they expected a pregnant woman to go to the bathroom often. After my third or fourth trip to the bathroom, I called Curtis into the room to tell him that I thought it was time to go to the hospital. I wanted him to remain calm. But he ran out of the bathroom, yelling, "It's time! It's time!" Everyone jumped up excitedly, hurrying to get the things I needed to go to the hospital. He loaded the kids and me into the van and began driving rapidly. We must have broken several traffic laws and probably put a few people's lives in danger, including our own. But, thank God, we arrived at the hospital safely and in record time.

After the nurse examined me, I was immediately wheeled into the delivery room. She obviously didn't realize how far along my labor was because she took her sweet time getting there, stopping on occasion to chat with other nurses. Much to her surprise, by the time she started to prep me for delivery, the baby was already coming. She was forced to deliver the baby by herself. Moments later, on Sunday, November 14, 1976, I gave birth to a healthy, six-pound fourteen-ounce baby girl. I named her Shameka Denee Crayon. My doctor finally arrived shortly afterwards to finish up the delivery procedures. As the nurse caught her breath, she asked me if I had heard of natural birth. I told her that I had. "Well, that sure is what you had," she said, panting.

I was in the hospital for about three days. Lots of friends and relatives visited our new bundle of joy and me. When we got back home, many of the van club members came by. They wondered if we should cancel the house party that was scheduled for Saturday. I told them that the party was still on. Our den was located at the rear of the house, away from the bedroom. So I didn't think it would be a problem to go on with the plans. I thought it would be more difficult to relocate the party. The party was a success. It was also the last van club party given at our house on Mayo Street.

Right after Shameka Denee was born, Curtis and I started having problems again. The arguments got so severe at times, I wished we had never gotten back together again. Many of our arguments centered around the fact that Curtis continued to have a relationship with a woman whom he had started seeing while we were separated. I had had a relationship with someone else during our separation that I eventually stopped because I didn't feel comfortable having the relationship around my children. On the other hand, Curtis didn't seem to know how to break off his relationship, so he continued to inconspicuously see her, even after we got back together. He allowed her to call our home, and she would even show up at our van parties. When I finally had had enough of Curtis' disrespecting our home and our relationship, I told him I wanted to break up for good.

Even after I decided to end the relationship, the children and I remained in the house on Mayo for a while, along with Curtis. He could tell that I was sincere. To be honest, I think he wanted the relationship to end as well. Despite that, he still tried to exercise control over me. He started monitoring the time I spent away from home and sometimes accused me of seeing someone. I guess he recalled the doggish things he had to do to cheat on me. I am sure that his conscious must have beaten the hell out of him to even think about me doing the same.

My supervisor at Austin Bradlee called to ask when I would be returning to work. They wanted me back as soon as possible and were willing to work around my schedule, considering I had a one-month-old baby. Because Curtis worked from 3:30 p.m. to midnight, I consented to work from 8:30 a.m. until 2 p.m. This way, Curtis would be home with Shameka, and I would get home before he left for work. If he needed to leave a few minutes before I got home, Andre and Tyree handled watching their baby sister.

Although I faithfully worked this schedule, I wasn't able to save very much money in order to move. After an argument with Curtis one weekend, I realized I had to find a better paying job if I was ever going to be able to get out of this situation. On that Monday, I called my supervisor and told him I would be absent for the rest of the week. I spent the entire week job-hunting. I applied at Panasonic and McDonnell Douglas Aircraft Company. At McDonnell Douglas, I took an aptitude test and a typing test. I failed the typing test by only a few words. Although I could type sixty words per minute and passing the test only required fifty words per minute, my nerves got the best of me, so I didn't type at my usual speed. I was offered a second chance, but I failed once again. The interviewer told me to go home and practice, then come back to take the test for the third time the following week.

By that Friday, I had applied for jobs with at least a dozen companies. I was bound and determined to land a better paying job. I also knew I could not continue to live with Curtis. I had to do better on the typing test on Monday. As soon as I arrived home that Friday afternoon, the telephone rang. It was a representative from Panasonic, offering me a job. I was prepared to start work on Tuesday at 8:30 a.m.

I spent the entire weekend considering my options. I decided to retake the typing test at McDonnell Douglas because the job there paid more and provided better benefits. Early Monday morning, I went back to McDonnell Douglas to take the test for the final time. My attitude was that if I passed it, I would get the job. If not, I still had the job waiting for me at Panasonic. Luckily, I passed the test. I was given a physical, took the picture for my badge, and was told to report to work on Wednesday. When I got home, I called Panasonic and told them that I had a better job offer and thanked them for considering me. I then started making preparations for my new job.

I began working at the Long Beach location of McDonnell Douglas as an Operations Control Analyst. After I had been employed approximately four months, the company moved me to the Torrance location for part of the day. They would send me from Long Beach at midday to Torrance, where I would do the same job. I was transported back to Long Beach at the end of the day. Then the company determined that it needed me to work all day at the Torrance location. And so, I spent the rest of my thirteen-year career with McDonnell Douglas, working at that location.

Although I spent a lot of time working, I still found time for my household chores and my children. There were many weekends I would have a house full of kids. All of my friends knew that I loved children and that I had no problems watching theirs. Andre and Tyree were not allowed to spend the night away from home too often, but I let their friends and relatives spend nights with them frequently.

Both boys had expressed some interest in karate, so I enrolled them in a martial arts school. I took them when I got off work in the evenings. Curtis didn't seem to like the idea of Andre and Tyree attending karate school (maybe he thought someday they might be able to beat him up). So, I never really told him that we were going. Each day they would bring their karate uniforms home, wash them, and hide them until the next day. Working full-time and then coming home, getting the baby ready, and taking the boys to karate everyday kept us busy, but we managed.

At McDonnell Douglas, I met Warren Griffin, one of the few Black men working in an upper-management position. We became good friends and spent many lunches and breaks together. We would share personal problems with one another and also had a few good laughs. He was nice and a good person to talk to. We enjoyed each other's company very much. There were a few other employees in our small circle at McDonnell Douglas that shared in the fun with us. It felt great to have a good job and be surrounded with good and positive people. I felt even more incentive to leave Curtis and develop a new lifestyle for my kids and me. I wasn't sure what I was waiting for at that point. I guess I was just too busy to get ready. And, since I felt Curtis wanted the move as well, I thought I could do it at any time.

Christmas came and went pretty uneventfully for me. The kids enjoyed themselves. I looked forward to going to a party at Curtis' brother, Donald's house with two of my girlfriends, Julia and Donna, on New Year's Eve. We planned to show our faces at the party and then leave. Right after the countdown into the

New Year, Julia, Donna, and I left the party. We needed to go to one of our homes to sit, talk, and enjoy the rest of the evening away from men because all of us were having man problems. We chose Julia's place.

She was living with Curtis' cousin, James. While we were sitting in her bedroom, I suddenly heard the sound of a muffler on a van. Neither Julia nor Donna heard anything. They both claimed that it was my imagination. We continued discussing our relationship problems when I heard someone at the door of the bedroom. Once again, I was the only one to hear it because the other girls were so busy talking that they only heard each other.

All of a sudden the bedroom door flew open and there stood James in the doorway. He calmly and politely asked Julia to come out for a minute. A few minutes after she left the room, we heard a loud clapping sound. After that, we heard Julia scream. Donna and I both stood up to go to her defense, but thought that doing so would be overstepping our boundaries. Julia never came back in the room. However, James made several trips into the room, never saying a word to us. He was carrying the dresser drawers from the room. When I finally went outside to see what was going on, I saw a pile of Julia's clothes in the front yard. James was taking the drawers and dumping her things there. Julia picked them up and neatly placed them in the trunk of her car.

I attempted to help her, but James asked me nicely to let her do it herself. To avoid further trouble, I obeyed his request and returned to the house. Donna and I decided after Julia was done packing, I would offer her to come stay at my house until she could find a place of her own. She was aware of my plans to leave Curtis and understood that her stay would be very short.

I suggested to Julia that she apply for a job at McDonnell Douglas. She did so and was hired right away. This worked out perfect for both of us. We would ride to and from work together and after work, we would search for apartments and houses to rent. We found a house for rent in Carson, near Avalon and Victoria Street. The house was in pretty bad shape, but it was affordable and was located approximately fifteen minutes from our job. It was a three-bedroom, two-bathroom house with a large backyard and patio.

For three weeks every evening after we got off work and picked up Andre and Tyree, we would go to work on the house for a few hours. The boys didn't mind missing karate because they were excited about moving to our new house. A few of the guys from work helped us out with the heavy work. This included Warren, whose friendship had blossomed into an intimate relationship. He helped with the painting and other tasks. Julia and I successfully completed the tasks that were necessary to make the house a decent and comfortable place to live—cleaning carpet; painting the entire house inside and out; adding missing doorknobs, switch plates, and light fixtures; fixing pipes in one bathroom; putting ceramic tile on the bathroom wall and floor; stripping the paint off the kitchen cabinets and staining them; replacing the tile on the kitchen floor; installing the missing sliding glass door in the kitchen; re-screening the patio; and having the junk hauled away from the backyard. People who saw the house in its beginning stages could not believe the finished product. They especially could not believe that two women nearly rebuilt and made what was a run-down place a nice house to live in.

After all that work, we only lived in the house for approximately six months. We moved after the owner refused to fix the plumbing problem. I moved back to my parents' house for a short time. Julia moved in with her new friend, Robert. Shortly after the kids and I moved back to my parents' house, Warren discussed with me the possibility of the two of us buying a house together. I thought it was a good idea since Warren and I had so much in common and he seemed so interested in my well-being.

Andre eight & Tyree five.

CHAPTER 14

Marriage with Warren

arren and I searched for a house and eventually settled on one located on Thorson Street, in Compton. Before we made the final decision to buy the house, we observed the neighborhood and its surroundings for two weeks in the evenings, mornings, and weekends. We saw one kid the whole time. We were overwhelmed by the quiet, peaceful atmosphere and decided to take the house.

After we moved in, we discovered that the neighborhood was *full* of kids. Kids seemed to have come out of the woodwork. And, they all enjoyed hanging out at our house. My children were very friendly and well-liked throughout the neighborhood. Andre was a magnet for kids. He seemed to get along well with everyone. Tyree was also a very friendly person who attracted kids in several age groups. Shameka had her own group of friends as well.

Warren and I decided that we wanted his only son, Warren III, better known as "Little Warren," to live with us. However, his ex-wife would have no part of that after she found out that his dad and I were living together. I assumed it was because she didn't want another woman raising her child. Warren had four children—three girls and a boy. Together, we managed to blend together seven children. Warren was very fond of his children and spent a lot of time with them.

After living together and attempting to consolidate our two families, we began talking about getting married. While it is said that, "The third time is the charm," I wasn't so sure about that. Warren and I had many problems that we needed to iron out. He was a wonderful person with a good heart and good intentions. However, at times, he did extra things for his kids, which presented an overwhelming financial problem for us. There was obvious jealousy on the part of the children's mother. She seemed to use the kids to make problems for us. I tried to be a trooper and continued to do what was needed to maintain our lifestyle. However, it was very difficult for us to take care of our own obligations since so much money was going out of the household to support Warren's kids.

I thought a lot about how much I had invested in the house we had just purchased together. I didn't want it to be another mistake. We had a few debates about how we could try to combat the problems we were having with our children, his children's mother, and the finances. We set guidelines to make each other feel more comfortable about dealing with the other's kids.

We also established a budget so that we would feel more financially stable. After things started to flow a little better, we decided to go ahead with the wedding plans. I wanted a small, simple wedding with just the two of us; he wanted a big wedding with everyone present. I gave into his desire to have a big wedding so long as we could keep the cost low. All of our kids were going to be in the wedding, along with Warren's brother George, my cousin Lois, and a friend Rose. To keep the cost to a minimum, we did most of the work ourselves. I made my dress and all of the bridesmaids' dresses. We were able to get the invitations at a good deal, and my friends and I cooked the food for the reception. The wedding and the reception came off without a hitch, and we received lots of compliments.

Shortly after we were married, Warren came home from work and told me that McDonnell Douglas plant workers were planning to go on strike. This was not good news at all. We knew that he needed to work and felt that crossing the picket line was not a good idea. The strike went on for over a month, causing our finances to suffer. We were behind on all of our bills. When the strike was finally over and Warren had returned to work, his department began laying off workers. We were very worried at that point. We also had another challenge. Warren had an old knee injury that flared up and gave him excruciating pain at times. He went out on medical leave right before he was scheduled to be laid off of work. Weeks passed before he received any money from his disability benefits. But at least he could expect income that went back to when he first went out on medical leave. And, fortunately, he was bypassed for the layoff.

Warren was paying child support and also providing additional money for the kids' necessities that their mother wasn't providing. While it wasn't fair that she wasn't living up to her responsibilities, he had no choice but to take care of his kids, whom he loved so much. We could not let them go without the things they needed because of her. We struggled financially, with seemingly no way of reducing our financial burden. In addition, we had the added responsibility of his son, Little Warren, who had started to spend more time in our home despite his mom's objections.

When Little Warren stayed weekends, he would cry when it was time to go home. So we started allowing him to stay during the week. Because it was summer, school was not an issue. Eventually, he stayed with us everyday. When the summer ended, we asked if Little Warren could stay with us permanently. His mother reluctantly consented and was probably greatly relieved to have one less mouth to feed.

With children, the end of summer is like the beginning of another year. We have to be concerned about school schedules, school clothes, lunches, and homework. In my case, it caused me to reflect on what I had gotten my kids and me into with Warren's kids and their mother. His sudden reduction in income made me wonder if my dream of providing a happy life for my kids would ever come true. I was beginning to feel that I had "jumped out of the skillet into the fire" by marrying Warren. The idea of bringing my kids from one struggle into another made me very unhappy.

Somehow I had to find a way to prevent myself from becoming a three-time loser in marriage. I constantly assured my children that everything was going to be alright.

One evening, the mother of Warren's children came to our house, demanding more money. A confrontation ensued, and she pulled a knife on Warren. She upset everyone, including the kids. I asked her to leave my house, but she refused. Shameka and Little Warren were crying hysterically. Tyree was trying to take the kids out of the room before they got hurt. It was a mess. After she said she didn't give a damn about upsetting the kids, I left the room and went to the porch to get an iron. By the time I got back, she had cut Warren's hand. I swung the iron at her, hitting her in the head. She immediately fell to the floor. Fortunately for her and me, I came to my senses and didn't hit her again. As she headed for the door, I tried to talk to her about her actions. I don't know if what I said was received because we were both so angry. But she did leave the house.

Andre & Daughter (La Tonya Young).

CHAPTER 15

Andre's Activities

ndre entered Centennial High School that year. I vowed to keep a close watch on his school performance to avoid the problems we had experienced the year before. He seemed to be doing quite well, as far as going to school everyday and maintaining decent grades. He was like most students—he excelled in some subjects and was just average in other subjects.

Andre's favorite class was drafting. His drafting instructor wanted him to enroll in an apprenticeship program at Northrop Aviation Company, but his grades in some of the other subjects were not good enough. Unfortunately, not being able to take advantage of this opportunity seemed to have a negative effect on him and his grades. I became really concerned and started discussing changing schools, thinking that a change of scenery might help. I allowed him to attend Fremont High School, in Los Angeles, where Curtis' youngest brother Darryl went. Curtis' mother allowed us to use her address.

Now that he was in high school, girls became a part of Andre's life. The first name that I heard him mention around the house was Lisa. Lisa lived in Culver City and was attending school out of her district as well. I never met her in person, but I did have one or two brief telephone conversations with her. She invited Andre and one of his friends over for an Easter celebration at her house once. I dropped them off, and her mother brought them back home. I guess I could have met Lisa then, but it just didn't seem to be that important at the time.

Not long after that, Lisa called and asked me if she could come to our house to visit Andre. After careful consideration, I agreed. A few minutes later, her mom called to say that Lisa was too young to be courting. I had assumed she had called with her mother's permission. We each agreed to talk to our children. We had a somewhat cordial conversation to discuss how the very ones you don't want your kids to see are the ones they tend to want to see. Teenagers have a natural need to defy authority, especially when it comes to relationships.

One day, I received *that phone call*—the call that all moms of teenagers dread, especially moms of teenaged boys. Lisa's mom called to inform me that Andre had been sneaking over to their house, and that Lisa was now pregnant. I didn't even know Andre was seeing Lisa, much less going to her home to have sexual relations with her. When I asked her if she was sure that it was Andre who had been with Lisa, she got very upset.

She said, "If I had come home and caught that nigger in my house, you would have been picking him up in a box." Needless to say, the conversation went downhill from there. I understood her anger, but she was talking about my son. I couldn't maintain my composure. When someone's making a threat on your child, regardless of the circumstances, that's just not something that you want to hear. I became defensive and told her that if she had harmed my son, there would have been no place that she could hide that I could not have found her.

I finally brought the discussion back to her daughter. "My son didn't break in your house and rape your daughter; she let him in, which makes her just as much at fault as he is," I said. We finally hung up. Even though we were both angry, we realized that we had the baby to think about.

Andre and I again had a long talk, but this time it was about him being a father. He listened for a long time and finally admitted to having sex with Lisa. I told him that I wanted him to do right for the baby, but I didn't suggest he get married, like my parents had forced me to do. After all, he was only seventeen, and Lisa was only sixteen. On January 19, 1983, a baby girl, La Tanya Danielle Young, was born. Lisa's mother would not let Andre see Lisa. We were not at the hospital the day the baby was born. But Andre managed to see his new baby girl in the hospital after she was born. I bought an assortment of baby items and sent them to Lisa. After a few months passed, Lisa brought the baby to our house for our family to see. I was 33 years old and already a grandmother.

I encouraged Andre to finish school so that he wouldn't run into the same problems that I did by missing out on his education. Needless to say, he started having the same problems at Fremont that he had experienced at the other schools. He also began ditching classes again. I presumed that he did so to be with Lisa. We went through battle after battle about his attendance at school and his grades. As before, the classes he liked, he excelled in, and the classes he didn't like, his grades suffered. His swimming instructor begged me to do what I could to help Andre bring his grades up. Andre was his best diver, but he couldn't remain on the swim team unless his grade point average was C or better. His English teacher said, "I know he's not a dummy; I watch him play chess at lunch time, and he beats everybody." She continued, "Students line up to challenge him, yet he remains undefeated." I didn't know what else to do. I thought I had done all that I could. I let him go to the school of his choice; I talked with him continuously; I talked to his teachers. I even threatened him. Yet, nothing seemed to work.

I wondered if I had been too easy on Andre. I questioned whether my relationship problems had affected my children. Before we could get the problem resolved, Andre had turned nineteen and became too old to attend high school. I felt that I had failed my child. I knew how important being a high school graduate was to my son's success.

Because I always wanted the best for my children, I also had some "tough love" rules. One such rule was that if you lived under my roof, you had to be productive. You either had to be going to school or working or both. Well aware of my rule, Andre came home to tell me that he had enrolled himself in Chester Adult School, in Compton. I asked him how he expected to do well in that school if he hadn't done well in regular school. He simply said, "The people who go to this school don't act crazy." I concluded that his failure at school related to seeing so much craziness at home. He didn't want to deal with the same craziness at school that he had to deal with at home.

Andre always managed to hold himself together at home. He remained calm, cool, and collected. His way of rebelling had been at school. I wondered how a child who had seen so much growing up managed to remain out of trouble, for the most part. I guess that some of my poor choices had taken their toll on my son. His failing school was one of those ways.

Andre excelled at Chester Adult School. He decided to go on to a broadcast school. We had to scrape up the money for him to go. I took him to the school for his first day of orientation and spent more than half the day with him. After orientation, he decided that he didn't want to go there after all. He said he felt as though the school was more about getting rich than helping students gain skills. He didn't want to risk my money on something that he didn't have a positive feeling about. While I was disappointed, I was also thankful to him for making such an unselfish decision. Still, I wanted him to find something positive to do with his life. I refused to let him be idle. I constantly encouraged him to look for a job.

Andre was never comfortable with our lifestyle, although he never mentioned that to me until the day he decided that he wanted to go stay with my parents. He never liked being amongst confusion, and there was so much of that in our house, especially concerning money.

After he left, I kept in constant contact with him, trying to convince him to come back home. I knew he was in good hands at my parents' house, even though my dad would sometimes get a little grouchy. I always thought my dad wanted Andre to live there. Andre soon left their house, got in touch with his dad, and went to stay with him for a very short time. His dad was still a drug dealer, even when Andre was living there. Theodore got arrested while Andre was there, but luckily, Andre was not at home during that time. Theodore's youngest sister Debra brought Andre back home and told us what had happened. While I hated hearing about Theodore's troubles, I was glad to have my son back at home, unharmed. I tried hard to keep the peace in my home so that Andre would not leave again.

Soon after moving back home, he took up an interest in dance. He and two of his friends, Darrin and "June Bug," started a dance group. At the time, a dance called *The Pop Lock* was popular. Andre and his dance group competed in many contests, but never finished any higher than second place. He quickly got tired of losing and decided to pick up deejaying, something that he felt he was good at and had enjoyed as a child.

In 1984, Andre asked for a music mixer for Christmas. He wanted to attach it to his amplifier and two turntables, which would allow him to repeat a chosen part of a record without skipping the beat. Warren and I did all we could to see to it that we as a family enjoyed a wonderful Christmas. We made sure that each one of our seven kids got at least one thing that they asked for out of the many gifts that we bought for them.

We spent most of Christmas Eve preparing Christmas dinner, entertaining company, and wrapping gifts. It had become a tradition for friends to gather at our house on Christmas Eve. Like many families, Warren and I wrapped gifts for most of the night. Doing that for seven children took a lot of time. Warren managed to have all his kids at our house for Christmas. By the time we went to sleep, the kids were ready to wake up. In fact, before we actually got to sleep, the kids were knocking at the door, anxious to see their gifts.

Andre was so excited when he unwrapped his mixer. He immediately got dressed and went out to show some of his friends before setting it up. He remained in his room all day, practicing with his mixer. I had to beg him to take a break just to eat.

That night after all of the guests had left and the other kids had all gone to sleep, I went into Andre's room to check on him. He was lying on his bed fast asleep, with his headsets still on his head and the music blasting. I took the headsets off, turned off the music, and threw a blanket over him, trying hard not to disturb his sleep. From that day forward, Andre took his place as the music person of our household.

At times, some of the neighbors would complain about the loud music. I would tell them that I was glad to hear the music because I always knew where my children were. I reminded them that they were not breaking in houses or sneaking up on people to knock them over the head. "If you take my children's music away from them, what will they have to do?" was my reasoning.

My house became party central. Just about every kid on the block would come by at some point during the day. This was a good thing as far as I was concerned. Their parents knew where to find them, and the kids respected my family and me.

The neighbors were right about one thing—the music was really loud. Sometimes I would walk through my house, yelling at the top of my lungs just so I could be heard over the music. Knowing that my kids were home safe made the noise bearable. *It was a fair trade*, I thought.

As evident by the wonderful Christmas we had, our financial situation began to improve, in part because Warren was getting more hours at work. After we were finally able to buy new furniture, I put the old furniture in our two-car garage, along with a refrigerator. This became the new spot for the kids to hang out. Warren, who was a third-degree black belt in the art of Shotokan karate, would sometimes hold karate classes for the boys in the garage. (In fact, Warren had once trained with Chuck Norris. Also, the same instructor that taught at the karate school where Andre and Tyree had taken lessons practiced with Warren.)

Despite the challenges of merging two families together, Warren and I had many good memories in our house on Thorson Street. Our kids seemed never to stray too far away from the house except to go to school, so I didn't have to worry much about them. Tyree attended Roosevelt Junior High School, and Shameka attended Mark Twain Elementary. Little Warren, who spent most of his time at our house, continued to go to school in the area where his mother lived.

Tyree experienced some problems at school with fighting. I frequently visited the school and became concerned for his safety because of the large number of teenagers who were involved in gangs. These gang members placed little or no value on human life. I didn't want Tyree caught up in that mess.

Tyree sometimes wore a pair of red pants that were the source of many of his fights. This was the beginning of the "red and blue color wars" of the gangs. He insisted that *no one* would dictate what he wore.

One day I was in the house doing my evening cleaning when I heard Tyree at a distance, frantically yelling out to me. I ran to the door and saw him running up the driveway, wearing those red pants and a group of boys chasing him. I opened the screen door and Tyree slid into the house as if he were sliding into home plate at a baseball game. I immediately grabbed the brass umbrella stand that was by the door and started swinging it. The group of boys attempted to follow him in the house until they saw me. They immediately backed off and ran away. Later that evening, I went into Tyree's room, found those red pants, and threw them in the trash. He never knew what happened to them.

Andre always tried to give Tyree the rules of survival. But Tyree was a defiant child and was determined that no one was going to tell him what to do. He was a good-hearted kid, although he maintained a tough exterior. Andre, on the other hand, was always very low-key, but he knew how to hold his own when he had to. Both of them had many friends who were gangbangers. I never ordered them to stay away from their friends because I didn't want to make them seem better than anyone. I taught them that no one was better than they were, and that they were no better than anyone else, just as my mom had taught me. When I saw them with people that had undesirable ways, I would call their attention to the possible consequences and issue a warning. I allowed my kids to make most of their own decisions. But they knew that if they made the wrong decision, they had to face punishment from me, which they hated with a passion.

One of Andre's best friends was a kid named Eric, who lived a few blocks from us on Muriel Street. Andre spoke of Eric in glowing terms, often bragging about the nice material things he had. When I asked Andre where Eric worked, he told me that he did not work. Because I had had my share of experiences with men who engaged in illegal activity, I immediately became suspicious of Andre's new friend. I was worried more than anything that Andre would be drawn to the glitter of what drug money could buy. I often told him, "Fast money is not good money." I warned him about the kinds of people it brings and the discomfort it causes from having to look over your shoulder and constantly watch your back. I explained that it was better to live with legal income that trickles in slowly than to deal with the madness that fast money brings, including the possibility of being killed.

Andre and a few of his friends formed a deejay group called *The Freak Patrol*. They would deejay at dances in a park around the corner from our house, as well as at club dances and house parties. Occasionally, I would take Andre, Tyree, and their friends to a club called *Eve after Dark*, which was a teen club that allowed the kids to showcase their talent on weekends. I would pile as many kids as I could fit in my car (of course, this was before the seatbelt law became effective) and would drive them to the club at about nine o'clock. I would return home and set my alarm clock for one o'clock in the morning, the time that I went back to the club to pick them up.

Andre hoped that going to the club would give him the opportunity to showcase his deejaying skills. One night, he was given the opportunity to do so when his godmother's brother, Tim, convinced the club owner to let him show his skills with the turntables. I wish I could have been there to support him, but the club was for young adults. I never dreamed that one chance to showcase his talent would mark the beginning of a musical legacy. That night when Andre got home, he was so excited as he told me that he had deejayed, and that the crowds loved it. That club gave Andre his first big break in what would be a very successful career. I didn't know that at the time. I was simply pleased that he had found something that held his attention and kept him out of trouble.

Shortly thereafter, Andre began calling himself "Dr. Dre, the Master of Mixology." He came up with the "Dr." part from his basketball idol, Dr. J. A few weeks after his debut as a deejay, as Andre walked near his grandparents' house, Lonzo, the manager of Eve after Dark, approached him and asked if he was the man people called Dr. Dre. When Andre responded, "yes," Lonzo offered him a job as the club's deejay, earning fifty dollars per night. Andre accepted the job offer and prepared to start immediately. When he told me about his new job, I was as excited as he was.

Before long, Andre realized he needed more than fifty dollars a night to make ends meet. During the day, he would hang out at the club with Lonzo and a few of their friends. After a while, he began noticing some recording equipment. Andre suggested that they try to do some recording. Although Lonzo thought it was a wild idea, he agreed to it. The idea eventually proved to be a pretty good one.

Andre and his friends put together a group called, *The World Class Wreckin' Cru*. This group consisted of Dr. Dre, Lonzo, D.J. Yella, Clientele, and Mona Lisa. Their first record was entitled, "Turn Off the Lights." Even though Andre and the group were selling records, he always seemed to be broke. I couldn't understand why he was constantly asking for loans. Later I found out that the group's manager had purchased a new house and a car, while Andre and the rest of the group were pulling out their pocket linings. Apparently the money was not filtering down to all the band members. Eventually the group disbanded.

After all those worries about schools, gangs, bad choices of friends, and sleepless nights, I was pleased that my son had found a career. I was happy that Andre was settling into something he enjoyed and hoped that it would one day be profitable for him. I never imagined just how profitable it would come to be. Andre Romell Young made his mark in the music industry and was soon to make the name *Dr. Dre* a musical legacy.

All of the struggles, scandals, fear of failure, and discouragement could be laid to rest. We would soon be living far better than we had ever lived before.

I loved all my children very much, for they all had a special quality. Tyree was my child that kept me laughing, even when I was feeling down or angry; Shameka was my only daughter and my baby; my stepchildren—Felicia, Traci, Mitzi, and Warren III—

didn't play a big part in my life, but taught me a lesson in how to be understanding. There was a lot of "tough love" going on, but I learned to be patient with them. I always say, "You have to know me to understand me, and you have to understand me to know me." I think that this theory would work well amongst all the races. Just think what a beautiful world this would be with a little more understanding.

Last, but not least, is Andre. Andre's qualities are many. He is my miracle child and my oldest son. He also seemed to hold the spot as the man in our family when there wasn't one present. We all looked up to Andre. He made my hopes and dreams of not being labeled as a failure come true just to see him (and my other children) succeed. This is what I had worked so hard for. He has continued to support his family and made life a lot easier for all of us. I can truly say if I die tomorrow, I feel that I have lived a wonderful life ... and it has been a *Privilege to Live* to see all of this happen.

WORLD CLASS WRECKIN' CRU

This is a picture of the group that Andre made his start into the world of music. From left to right: Lonzo, D. J. Yella, Dr. Dre, Shakespeare, and the young lady in the back, Mona Lisa, sang on a few of their records.

Privileged to Live

After all that's said and done, I truly was the one
The secondary clown that they
Loved to have around
To do the things they do, to argue the fact "who
do"
Never coming to a conclusion of
What started this confusion
Simply casting it aside, while my feelings I try to
hide
Drowning in alcohol and such convincing myself
that I
Loved that much
After the hangover is over
Facing the same problems sober
Growing bigger day by day
As the years go by, the problems stay
Thoughts of ending it all through self-infliction
is such
A cowardly conviction
This would surely hurt the ones who care
To hurt them is a burden I cannot bear
Through my trials and tribulations
I know God has been my salvation
I know I've had God on my side
Someone has protected me and kept me alive
And it truly is a **Privilege to Live**

—Verna Griffin

BOOK AVAILABLE THROUGH
Milligan Books, Inc.

"Privileged to Live"
Price: $21.95

Order Form

Milligan Books, Inc.
1425 W. Manchester Ave., Suite C, Los Angeles, CA 90047
(323) 750-3592

Name_____ Date _____

Address _____

City_____State_____ Zip Code_____

Day Telephone_____

Evening Telephone_____

E-Mail_____

Book Title_____

Number of books ordered_____ Total $_____

    Sales Taxes (CA Add 8.25%) $_____

    Shipping & Handling $4.90 for one book $_____

    Add $1.00 for each additional book $_____

    Total Amount Due $_____

    ☐ Check   ☐ Money Order   ☐ Visa   ☐ MasterCard

    ☐ Other Cards _____Expiration Date _____

Credit Card No ._____

Driver License No. _____

    Make check payable to Milligan Books, Inc.

Signature _____ Date _____